Semantic Technologies in Content Management Systems

Wolfgang Maass • Tobias Kowatsch
Editors

Semantic Technologies in Content Management Systems

Trends, Applications and Evaluations

Editors

Prof. Dr.-Ing. Wolfgang Maass
Chair in Business Administration,
esp. Information and Service Systems
Saarland University
P.O. 15 11 50
66041 Saarbrücken, Germany
wolfgang.maass@iss.uni-saarland.de
www.iss.uni-saarland.de

Tobias Kowatsch, M.Sc.
Institute of Technology Management
Dufourstrasse 40a
9000 St. Gallen, Switzerland
tobias.kowatsch@unisg.ch
www.item.unisg.ch

ISBN 978-3-642-21549-0　　　　e-ISBN 978-3-642-24960-0
DOI 10.1007/978-3-642-24960-0
Springer Heidelberg Dordrecht London New York

Library of Congress Control Number: 2011941494

© Springer-Verlag Berlin Heidelberg 2012

This work is subject to copyright. All rights are reserved, whether the whole or part of the material is concerned, specifically the rights of translation, reprinting, reuse of illustrations, recitation, broadcasting, reproduction on microfilm or in any other way, and storage in data banks. Duplication of this publication or parts thereof is permitted only under the provisions of the German Copyright Law of September 9, 1965, in its current version, and permission for use must always be obtained from Springer. Violations are liable to prosecution under the German Copyright Law.

The use of general descriptive names, registered names, trademarks, etc. in this publication does not imply, even in the absence of a specific statement, that such names are exempt from the relevant protective laws and regulations and therefore free for general use.

Printed on acid-free paper

Springer is part of Springer Science+Business Media (www.springer.com)

Contents

Part I Introduction to Content Management Systems and Semantic Technologies

1 On the Changing Market for Content Management Systems: Status and Outlook 3
Wolfgang Maass
 1.1 Introduction 3
 1.2 Content Management Systems 4
 1.3 Outlook 6
 References 7
 Biographical Notes 7

Part II Editorial – The Future of Content Management Systems

2 Empowering the Distributed Editorial Workforce 11
Steve McNally
 2.1 Introduction 11
 2.2 CMS Expectations: Philosophy and Tools 12
   2.2.1 In-Line Editing 13
   2.2.2 Semantic Tools and Contextual Presentation 14
   2.2.3 Curation Tools 16
 2.3 Roles, Rights and Reputation 18
   2.3.1 Definition of Role 18
   2.3.2 Basic Roles and Rights 19
   2.3.3 Reputation 19
 2.4 Conclusion 21
 References 22
 Biographical Notes 22

3 The Rise of Semantic-aware Applications ... 23
Stéphane Croisier
- 3.1 Introduction ... 23
- 3.2 First Challenge: Easing the Connections with Smart and Trusted Information Warehouses ... 24
- 3.3 Second Challenge: Automating the Semantic Geekery ... 25
- 3.4 Third Challenge: Delivering Compelling Information Experiences ... 29
- 3.5 Future of CMS: Fostering Rapid Development and Assembly of Semantic-aware Applications ... 29
- 3.6 Conclusion ... 32
- References ... 32
- Biographical Notes ... 33

4 Simplified Semantic Enhancement of JCR-based Content Applications ... 35
Bertrand Delacretaz and Michael Marth
- 4.1 Introduction ... 35
- 4.2 Use Cases for Semantic Content Enhancement and Search ... 36
  - 4.2.1 Core Language Help for Content Authors ... 36
  - 4.2.2 Putting Content in the Context of Other Content Items ... 36
  - 4.2.3 Putting Content in the Context of the Real World ... 37
  - 4.2.4 User-generated Content ... 37
  - 4.2.5 Semantic Image Similarity ... 38
  - 4.2.6 The Semantic Engine as an Assistant – Not a Master ... 38
- 4.3 Missing Pieces ... 39
  - 4.3.1 Content Enhancement Engine ... 39
  - 4.3.2 Semantic Metadata Storage ... 40
  - 4.3.3 Semantic Queries ... 40
  - 4.3.4 User Interfaces ... 40
- 4.4 JCR-Based Implementation ... 41
  - 4.4.1 JCR Storage Model: Nodes, Properties and Node Types ... 41
  - 4.4.2 JCR Micro-trees and Content Trees ... 41
  - 4.4.3 Semantic Metadata in Micro-trees ... 43
  - 4.4.4 Simplified Semantic Queries ... 44
  - 4.4.5 Searching for Semantic Annotations ... 44
  - 4.4.6 Searching for Pages that Reference a Given Entity or Set of Entities ... 45
  - 4.4.7 Searching for Related Pages ... 45
  - 4.4.8 Is it that Simple? ... 45
  - 4.4.9 Mapping RDF Triples to our Simplified Notation ... 46
- 4.5 Closing Comments ... 46
  - 4.5.1 Risks and Challenges ... 46
  - 4.5.2 Semantic Content Enrichment and Mining in CMS ... 47
- 4.6 Conclusion ... 47
- References ... 47

			Biographical Notes	48
5	**Dynamic Semantic Publishing**			49
	Jem Rayfield			
	5.1	Introduction		50
	5.2	Static Publishing and CPS CMS		51
	5.3	Dynamic Semantic Annotation Driven Publishing		54
	5.4	Fully Dynamic Publishing		61
	5.5	Conclusion		64
		Biographical Notes		64
6	**Semantics in the Domain of eGovernment**			65
	Luis Álvarez Sabucedo and Luis Anido Rifón			
	6.1	Introduction		65
	6.2	The Domain		66
	6.3	Existing Approaches to eGovernment		67
		6.3.1	Governmental Initiatives	67
		6.3.2	Standardization Bodies	68
		6.3.3	Projects in the Domain	69
	6.4	Introducing Semantics in eGovernment Solutions		70
		6.4.1	Annotating Documents	70
		6.4.2	Describing Services	71
		6.4.3	Social Services	71
	6.5	Conclusion		71
		References		72
		Biographical Notes		73
7	**The Interactive Knowledge Stack (IKS): A Vision for the Future of CMS**			75
	Wernher Behrendt			
	7.1	Introduction		75
	7.2	1970 to 1990: Relational Databases, Object-Orientation and AI ...		76
	7.3	1990 to 2000: From Altavista to Google – Post HOC Search Wins Over A Priori Structure		77
	7.4	Critical Appraisal of the Search Metaphor in View of Content Management		78
	7.5	Operating Systems, Web Communities and the Biggest CRM Database Ever Built		79
	7.6	From Large Scale Customer Acquisition Engines to Business-Related Content Management		80
	7.7	Critical Appraisal of the Semantic Web – We Need Technology Stacks, Not Language Cakes		81
	7.8	Strategic Positioning and Main Elements of IKS		83
		7.8.1	Addressing CMS Providers	84
		7.8.2	The Interactive Knowledge Stack (IKS)	84
		7.8.3	Knowledge-based Interaction with Content	85

	7.8.4	Technologies for Semantic Content Management	86
	7.8.5	A Reference Architecture for IKS	86
	7.8.6	RESTful Services for Integration with Existing CMS	87
	7.8.7	BSD-based Open Source Approach to Ensure Re-use without Constraints	87
7.9		Conclusion – Research Follows Industry in the Interest of Impact	87
References			89
Biographical Notes			90

8 Essential Requirements for Semantic CMS ... 91
Valentina Presutti

8.1		Introduction	91
8.2		Semantic Web Essential Requirements for CMS	94
	8.2.1	Integrity Check of External Data: A Scenario for Semantic CMS	94
8.3		KRES: Towards for CMS Essential Requirements	101
	8.3.1	Ontology Network Manager (ONM)	102
	8.3.2	Semion	102
	8.3.3	Rule and Inference Manager (RIM)	104
8.4		Related Work	104
8.5		Conclusion	105
References			106
Biographical Notes			107

Part III Evaluation and Profiles of 27 CMS Provider Companies

9 Evaluation of Content Management Systems ... 111
Tobias Kowatsch and Wolfgang Maass

9.1		Introduction	111
9.2		Methodology	112
9.3		Results	120
9.4		Profiles of CMS Provider Companies	121
	9.4.1	CMS with No Specific Industry Focus	122
	9.4.2	CMS with a Specific Industry Focus	123
References			123
Biographical Notes			123

10 CMS with No Particular Industry Focus ... 125

10.1	Alfresco, United Kingdom: Alfresco	126
10.2	Alkacon Software GmbH, Germany: OpenCms	128
10.3	Brunner AG, Druck und Medien, Switzerland: mirusys®	131
10.4	Day Software (now part of Adobe), Switzerland: CQ5	133
10.5	Dynamic Works, Cyprus: EasyConsole CMS	136
10.6	EPiServer AB, Sweden: EPiServer CMS	139
10.7	Gentics Software GmbH, Austria: Gentics Content.Node	142

Contents ix

	10.8	GOSS Interactive Ltd, United Kingdom: GOSS iCM: intelligent Content Management 144
	10.9	Homepage Toolbox, Austria: Homepage Toolbox 147
	10.10	Jahia Solutions Group, Switzerland: Jahia 149
	10.11	Jarn AS, Norway: Plone 152
	10.12	Klein & Partner KG, BlueDynamics Alliance, Austria: Plone..... 155
	10.13	Magnolia International Ltd., Switzerland: Magnolia CMS 158
	10.14	MASSIVE ART WebServices GmbH, Austria: ZOOLU 161
	10.15	Modera, Estonia: Modera Webmaster........................ 164
	10.16	Nemein Oy, Finland: Midgard CMS......................... 167
	10.17	NexxaCon IT-Consulting GmbH, Austria: join2learn 170
	10.18	Nuxeo, France: NUXEO 172
	10.19	Ooffee, France: Apache Lenya 175
	10.20	punkt. netServices GmbH, Austria: conX 178
	10.21	semsol, Germany: Paggr CMS 180

11 CMS with a Particular Industry Focus 183

	11.1	CIC Creative Internet Consulting GmbH, Germany: packagemaster® 184
	11.2	Hippo B.V., The Netherlands: Hippo CMS 187
	11.3	PAUX Technologies GmbH, Germany: PAUX 190
	11.4	QuinScape GmbH, Germany: OpenSAGA 193
	11.5	TERMINALFOUR, Ireland: TERMINALFOUR: Site Manager... 195
	11.6	TXT Polymedia, Italy: TXT Polymedia....................... 198

Index 201

Part I
Introduction to Content Management Systems and Semantic Technologies

Chapter 1
On the Changing Market for Content Management Systems: Status and Outlook

Wolfgang Maass

1.1 Introduction

Almost 10 years ago, Content Management Systems (CMS) were already important tools for corporate communications on the web that supported key communication situations with consumers, investors, media people, and others [6]. Now Communication Management has become an integral and important part of any organization. But at the same time also individuals started to manage their online communication with technical tools other than just email. So-called social media provide individuals with content management capabilities that used to require larger technical installations and administration. Today, anybody can manage his own digital content space in real-time by a minimum of technical requirements – most of the time for free. Consequently contents grew with an unprecedented speed. In 2009 online content increased by about 60% to nearly 800,000 PetaBytes and is assumed to increase by factor 44 by 2020 [5].

In 2003, we found a trend that the larger a company the fewer people actively used a corporate CMS [7]. On the long tail end this view needs to be extended by more than 500 million users of Facebook who spend combined about 1.3 million years per month sharing more than 30 billion content objects per month (2010) (http://www.facebook.com/press/info.php?statistics). Furthermore Wikipedia supports 365 million readers (2009), 1,3 million editors with more than 10 contributions, 12.3 million edits, and on average 36 revisions per article (Dec. 2010) (http://stats.wikimedia.org/EN/Sitemap.htm) and Craigslist serves 20 billion page views (June 2010) and about 55 million unique users in the US alone (December 2010) (http://en.wikipedia.org/wiki/Craigslist).

Several challenges have been identified to cope with this amount of content [5]:

1. New search tools

Wolfgang Maass
Chair in Information and Service Systems (ISS), Faculty of Law and Economics, Saarland University, Germany, e-mail: wolfgang.maass@iss.uni-saarland.de

2. Ways to add structure to unstructured data
3. New storage and information management techniques
4. More compliance tools
5. Better security

While points 3 to 5 are standard issues for complex information technologies, points 1 and 2 are interesting from the point of CMS. The digital content space is only partially accessible via search engines, such as Google and Microsoft's Bing, and leaves large parts invisible (aka 'Deep Web'). This brings up the need for new search tools that might be based on federated search indexes, such as Katta (http://katta.sourceforge.net/). Hierarchical federation of distributed and interoperable search indexesSearch index!interoperable could provide a means for getting access to the Deep Web. Related is the second issue: add structure to unstructured data. Ever since the beginning of the World Wide Web, Timothy Berners-Lee had the idea of adding some kind of meaning to contents and their relationships [3]. Attempts were made to reuse results from Artificial Intelligence to this problem but also here Timothy Berners-Lee already argued for a more practical and large-scale approach based on the Resource Description Framework (RDF) [3]. Other lightweight semantic markup languages are microformats (http://microformats.org/) or RDFa (http://www.w3.org/TR/xhtml-rdfa-primer/). RDF and similar approaches help to create web-based semantic descriptions about digital contents (cf. Behrendt; Croisier; Delacretaz & Marth; Presutti; Rayfield in this book). This makes schematic information accessible via the Web at any time that is hidden in data models of relational databases at design time only. By leveraging the distributed design of the Web and in particular its addressing mechanism, Unified Resource Identifiers (URI), anybody can independently add anything about any topic [1]. This freedom has its price: if somebody wants to use a semantic description she has to understand what is meant by a particular name or relationship. Either meaning of descriptions is coded into standards, such as Dublin Core, or technological solutions for mapping and matching descriptions from different origins are used [4]. By departing from pure logical formalisms, it is quite common to use semi-structured sources as mediator, such as Wikipedia (dbpedia) or Wordnet for mapping unstructured contents to structured descriptions. These are not exact descriptions but are good enough ("satisficing") for most cases. This results in a two-layered system: digital contents and semantic annotations.

1.2 Content Management Systems

Developments on the long-tail side of CMS users means that Content Management is no longer just a topic for large organizations but also directly affects individual private users. In 2003 we found a CMS market that was fragmented into few categories [7]: Online CMS, Web CMS, Enterprise CMS, Cross Media CMS, and eLearning CMS. Today there are many categories in between and beyond.

Since that time, Open Source Software has become the standard technology platform for almost any non-commercial and commercial CMS. Beside traditional CMS providers, also service providers, such as Facebook, Google, and Yahoo heavily invest in Open Source Software solutions for their future content management services. Proprietary solutions are no longer flexible enough to respond in time to increasing market needs and technological innovations. Exceptions are large CMS provider, such as Microsoft, Open Text or Autonomy but also Enterprise CMS providers that integrate their CMS solutions deep into their business solutions, most of all IBM, Xerox, and Oracle.

CMS providers are forced to embrace social media services and to open their CMS solutions to content processing technologies opened up by Facebook, Google, and others. Strategically this puts a lot of pressure on CMS providers to keep track of technological developments that might become a death race for some CMS providers.

In summary, the CMS market can be dissected into three areas: (1) private market, (2) business market, and (3) big data market. The private market for CMS consists of small-scale CMS installations for private or small firms' use. This market shrinks by free or cheap online solutions offered by big data market providers. It might remain a test field for technology savvy people who want to learn and to innovate. Instead, small firms have either no web sites or tend to use portal sites. This long-tail market might become a future place of a fierce but short competition similar to Craigslist's takeover of the classified advertising market in the US.

The strong business market for CMS has grown in double digits till 2008 up to a revenue of $3.3 billion for Enterprise CMS in 2008 and with an expectation of about $5 billion in 2013 [2]. This market is currently changed by four drivers: (1) real-time commerce, (2) social media, (3) cost cutting by means of Open Source Software solutions, and (4) stronger adoption of Microsoft Sharepoint. Companies increasingly invest in solutions that help them to analyze customer behaviour on their web sites in real-time for instant customization of their offerings. Web communities, such as Facebook, provide tremendous insights for companies. Innovative solutions are required for leveraging these insights. Because social media push their introduced Open Source Software solutions very hard, it gives companies incentives for adopting these solutions. At the other end, Microsoft and its partners are also pushing hard for adoption of their CMS solutions based on Sharepoint for several years now. Further consolidation of CMS vendors is inevitable. Regulatory requirements are the strongest drivers for adopting commercial CMS solutions by medium and large companies. Incumbents, such as Microsoft and Oracle, possess capabilities for providing pre-configured CMS solutions geared towards those complex regulatory requirements that will give them a strategic advantage.

The big data market is nurtured by two trends. Currently the big data market is driven by social media platforms, such as Facebook and Youtube. Fast, super-large-scale and still reliable CMS solutions are developed and contributed to various Open Source Software projects that allow to (1) getting involved external contributors and ideas in the sense of Open Innovation and (2) bias world-wide thinking about big data solutions and thus setting de-facto standards similar to successful strategies for the flat panel display market (Spencer 2003). One option is that the big data market will create a global content infrastructure as a backbone for vertical content-driven applications. At least for Europe the likelihood of this option is increased by the fact that the European ICT industry is far behind in building data center for the big data market except some smaller scale 'private cloud' data centers. The second trends is more hidden and driven by healthcare industries and eGovernment activities (cf. Croisier; Sabucedo & Rifón in this book). For instance, huge data sets are created by genome projects while governments open up their data repositories for external use (e.g., http://data.gov.uk/sparql or http://www4.wiwiss.fu-berlin.de/factbook/snorql/).

1.3 Outlook

Some future challenges and trends for CMS solutions shall be given at the end as a starting point for discussions:

1. Deeper integration with core business solutions, in particular Enterprise CMS and Business Process Management solutions
2. Real-time responses to user activities by strong integration of real-time business intelligence in CMS solutions with solutions such as Apache Hive
3. Re-designing CMS architectures by leveraging of cloud service and big data infrastructures
4. Making contents meaningful by adding computational semantics, e.g. tags, taxonomies, and ontologies (cf. Behrendt; Croisier; Delacretaz & Marth; McNally; Presutti; Rayfield in this book)
5. Balancing between client and server-sided computations, e.g., client-sided and server-sided Javascript
6. Rise of 3D contents and 3D interaction spaces rendered at run-time, e.g. WebGL and holographics
7. Seamless integration of mobile content delivery infrastructures
8. Real-time integration and processing of large-scale sensor data
9. DynamicContent!dynamic, contextContent!context and user-adaptive content rendition (cf. McNally; Rayfield in this book)
10. Positioning CMS solutions within future browser/operating systems battles in mobile, cloud, and stationary infrastructures.
11. Long-term persistency and archiving of digital contents
12. Security of contents, CMS, and ICT channels
13. Global and unambiguous ownership of digital contents with full and barrier-free control for all those contents (cf. McNally in this book)
14. Breaking up content silos (cf. Croisier in this book)

It might be that we stand at the beginning of a new data explosion caused by sensors of various complexities and even more provisioning of personal data. High-quality selection and transformation of data into meaningful contents are some of the key challenges that will prevent us from drowning in data noise. In principle the digital World Wide Web infrastructure was meant to support sharing contents without any barriers. At the moment we are living in a world of huge content silos where even tiny content gateways are strongly protected and used as strategic weapons (e.g., http://www.wired.com/epicenter/2010/11/google-facebook-data/). A better digital world would force these silo providers to offer big gateways that allows for seamless sharing of contents as part of high-quality collaboration and communication but also as a basis for future innovations.

References

1. Allemang, D., James A. Hendler: Semantic Web for the Working Ontologist: Effective Modeling in RDFS and OWL. Morgan Kaufmann, Waltham, MA, USA (2008)
2. Bell, T., Shegda, K.M., Gilbert, M.R., Chin, K.: Magic quadrant for enterprise content management. Tech. rep., Gartner (2010)
3. Berners-Lee, T.: Information management: A proposal (1989). URL http://www.w3.org/History/1989/proposal.html
4. Euzenat, J., Shvaiko, P.: Ontology Matching. Springer, Heidelberg, Germany (2007)
5. IDC: The digital universe decade - are you ready? (2010). URL http://www.emc.com/collateral/demos/microsites/idc-digital-universe/iview.htm
6. Maass, W., Stahl, F.: Content Management als Teil des Kommunikations-Management. In: F. Stahl, W. Maass (eds.) Content Management Handbuch: Strategien, Theorien und Systeme für erfolgreiches Content Management, pp. 35–47. NetAcademy Press, St. Gallen, Switzerland (2003)
7. Stahl, F., Maass, W.: Content-Management-Handbuch: Strategien, Theorien und Systeme für erfolgreiches Content-Management. NetAcademy Press, St. Gallen, Switzerland (2003)

Biographical Notes

Wolfgang Maass holds a Chair in Information and Service Systems (ISS) at the faculty of Law and Economics of the Saarland University, Germany. Prior to that, he has led the Smart Products research group at the Institute of Technology Management (ITEM) at the University of St. Gallen, Switzerland and the Research Center for Intelligent Media (RCIM) at Furtwangen University, Germany. In 1996, he completed his Ph.D. in Computer Science at Saarland University. He was awarded with a habilitation in Business Administration with special focus on Information Management by the Department of Management at University of St. Gallen in 2007.

His research focuses on understanding design methodologies for complex Information Systems and in particular Ubiquitous Information Systems and Intelligent Information Systems. Emphasis is given to the analysis of full product design cycles, including creating and empirical evaluation of innovative Information Systems. His current interest is on the design of situated Information Systems by leveraging semantic technologies, multi-modal communication technologies, and technologies from the Internet of Things (IOT) and Internet of Services (IOS).

He is a member of the editorial board of Electronic Markets and a reviewer for the European Journal of Information Systems, Decision Support Systems, the International Journal on Media Management, and the Journal of Theoretical and Applied Electronic Commerce Research.

Part II
Editorial – The Future of Content Management Systems

Chapter 2
Empowering the Distributed Editorial Workforce

Steve McNally

Abstract The scope of Content Management Systems has expanded to include the entire ecosystem surrounding the creation, management and consumption of content. The definition of the editorial workforce has expanded, too, to include participants within and outside of traditional publishing organizations. Requirements for efficient interfaces, intention- and contextually-aware semantic tools in support of content creation, editing and interaction across multiple devices has grown in importance as they enable working effectively with the expanded scope of content and people interacting with the content being managed. Participants in the ecosystem each have their own sub-networks of friends, professional and academic contacts to whom they should be able to easily turn for insights, feedback and general participation. It is this enabling and leveraging of the network effect[1]: that helps achieve the growth and scale that is mutually beneficial to creators, editors, publishers, advertisers and community members.

2.1 Introduction

The people who use Content Management Systems (CMSs) each use the tools that make up the platform not only to manage content but also to build an experience. Those who experience these creations—the people formerly known as the audience [4]—are participants in the experience: they read, comment, and share what has been created, edited and curated.

Traditionally, CMSs were built around specific processes rather than around people. While reasonable systems need to be built around sets of tasks, workflows and rules, peoples' jobs usually encompass a number of disparate tasks. With regard to

---

Steve McNally
Senior Group Director, Editorial Tools & Product Development, Forbes Media, New York, USA,
e-mail: smcnally@forbes.com

[1] http://en.wikipedia.org/wiki/Network_effect

web content creators, editors, curators, these tasks span pages, sections and entire sites.

The modern CMS allows creators, editors and curators to interact with pages, sections and the whole site just as the general community does: Creators write posts, articles or comments. Editors can modify content of their own creation, sometimes that of others, and they can also package and promote content—slot it onto a home page, e.g., or into featured areas in a header or sidebar. Curators note that content is worthwhile by reading it, interacting with it, or sharing it. All community members view the same pages, but the creators, editors and curators have the ability to manipulate them.

Traditional roles are expanded. The editorial workforce is no longer centralized. Creators, editors and curators can be staffers, part-timers, or members of the community. Positive participation is rewarded with additional authority and capability.

Through it all is the on-going balancing act between high-function and intrusion. Much content and metadata regarding that content's relevance is presented within the context of what the creator or editor is viewing and doing. This relevance is contextual. It can always be requested explicitly. Opportunities are constantly sought to make contextually relevant content and information ambiently available so it shows up when it is natural for it to do so.

The modern CMS supports a community of participants. These participants interact with the content to varying degrees based on their permissions. All participants can be creators, editors, and curators. Following are details and use cases to demonstrate how this is accomplished.

The contribution of this chapter is intended to present works completed, works-in-progress and concepts yet to be realized with regard to the modern CMS. We will discuss the philosophy of tools designed to fit into organic workflows and to make relevant information available ambiently to creators and editors. Next, we discuss the roles involved in the creation of a decentralized editorial workforce empowered to attract, engage and grow an audience. Finally, we detail methods by which we engage, measure and reward credible, reputable contributions to the system and how the combination of all of the above streamlines and amplifies the process of content creation, management and interaction.

2.2 CMS Expectations: Philosophy and Tools

The modern CMS strives for frictionless publishing and promotion of content. The system is geared toward creating the shortest distance between creators' ideas and their publication. Removing layers between concept and publishing—between content and community—changes the mindset of working within the system: It transforms "tasks" into "work-style". It deepens and widens the pool of potential participants in the process.

Removing the need for creators and editors to go to a special place—a backend tool outside of the normal course of events for the majority of participants—creates a new norm for creators and editors. It removes some of the work and provides an ongoing perspective. The mindset of "working" changes as it becomes "looking at the site, seeing what's coming in, and seeing what's worth promoting and packaging."

The system enables a distributed editorial team comprised of staffers, part-timers, and engaged community members. They are each granted a role authorizing them to participate in specific, pre-defined tasks. They are given incentives to participate.

The tools create efficiencies in the creation, editing, and curation—selection, packaging and promotion—of content throughout the system.

2.2.1 In-Line Editing

In-line editing—also referred to as surf-and-edit—allows editorial team members to view site content as the general community does while also allowing them to update that content. Additional functionality beyond viewing is presented to authenticated members based on their role and authorization level. In-line editing provides context and perspective of how the content being edited will appear once those edits are published.

Use Case 1: Editor

> A member with the role of *Home Page Editor* will see additional links when visiting the home page. Story titles will be highlighted to note they are editable. Excerpts and images will have *Edit*, *Add New* and *Promote* link actions next to them. A *Re-arrange* link allows editors to drag and drop home page stories into a new order or to insert other content not currently present into the home page (see Fig. 2.1).

Working as a content creator or editor within the same context that community members are interacting with the content provides an on-going contextuality. From a tools perspective, subsuming the create and edit tools within the context of the final product removes a layer between editor and community: editors need not log into a separate area, traverse a file system or series of directory folders to find the file to edit and later publish. Rather, they work on the content in-line and in the same context the public will experience that content.

Practical advantages of role-based in-line editing also include mitigated training requirements. This enables a significant expansion of potential participants: as everyone is capable of visiting site pages that interest them, granularizing editorial capabilities down to the level of topics, sub-topics, and even keywords means publishers can recruit workforce members interested solely in "scratching their own

Fig. 2.1: In-line editing

itch"[2]: Community members care less about what the Publisher, e.g., wants; they are interested in what they want themselves. Some additional participation can be expected from the community when Publishers provide community members with what they are interested in seeing. Once interests and roles are defined, community members can be targeted down to the individual, and individuals can be grouped along lines of historical interests and activities. Members and groups can be catered to organically. Authorized community members can view, edit and curate topics, keywords or subjects in which they have vested interest. Individual itches can be scratched while still serving the good of the overall community.

Members of the community, through their own activities related to that content can become packagers and promoters implicitly via their engagement with the content and explicitly via rewards systems (more on that to come in Section *Roles, Rights* and *Reputation*). This empowers and engages community members. It provides a highly curated experience featuring quality content for the audience. It provides the publisher with a highly engaged and specialized workforce packaging and promoting content based on these individuals' subject matter interest and expertise.

2.2.2 Semantic Tools and Contextual Presentation

Providing basic categorical or taxonomic information for content allows that content to flow to appropriate areas of the system. Taxonomic metadata about content can be applied manually and explicitly by creators and editors or automatically and implicitly via algorithm.

Explicit taxonomic information includes when creators and editors manually add keywords and categories. Information can be added explicitly via first-hand knowledge of creators and editors or may be suggested by tools like Zemanta (http://

---

[2] http://en.wikipedia.org/wiki/The_Cathedral_and_the_Bazaar#Content

www.zemanta.com) or OpenCalais (http://www.opencalais.com) which process content as it is being created as well as after publication.

Implicit taxonomic information generally includes post-publish processing of content including the extraction and handling of known categories and entities.

Use Case 2: Creator

> Implicit information is added when occurrences of *Robert DeNiro*, *Lady Gaga* or *Steve Jobs* appear in content being created. These names are automatically marked-up and linked to profile pages from The Internet Movie Database (http://www.imdb.com), Gracenote (http://www.gracenote.com) and Forbes' Billionaires' Lists based on pre-defined rules (Fig. 2.2).

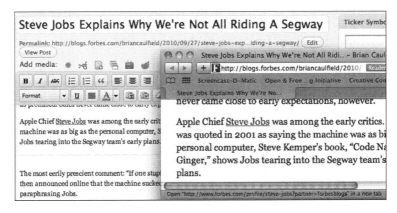

Fig. 2.2: Names are automatically marked-up and linked by semantic entity extraction

Extending the taxonomy provided by, e.g., the Open Directory Project (http://www.dmoz.org), to include publisher-specific information regarding entities and their appropriate linked pages allows publishers to extract those entities and link them to resources that create opportunities for additional revenues, Search Engine Optimization (SEO) benefits, and direct traffic while giving community members the opportunity to delve more deeply into subject maters of interest. The object being availing of cross-promotional opportunities, within and outside of the current content and site, while mitigating the need for explicit taxonomic work on the part of creators and editors: defined entity extraction rules, e.g., will link celebrity names, automatically, to a content partner specializing in Hollywood; the names of popular cultural figures will link to a sister-site specializing in music, culture and the arts, and the names of business figures will link to people and company profile information elsewhere on your own content network. Creators and editors will have the opportunity to change these automatically generated links; but, by default, unlinked entities will be discovered and linked to predefined sources without the need for further action on their parts.

2.2.3 Curation Tools

Curation is the act of noting certain content as worthwhile. All roles and community members can curate content, and curation can be explicit or implicit. First, explicit curation includes up-voting posts or comments—such as using the *Like*-button from Facebook (http://www.facebook.com)—leaving a comment, or sharing content via Facebook, Reddit (http://www.reddit.com) or elsewhere. Giving money to posts or comments with the help of micropayment services like Flattr (http://flattr.com) would be another example for explicit curation.

Second, implicit curation includes clicking through to an article or comment, spending active time on that content (e.g. time on page plus scrolling past preconfigured checkpoints within the content). It can include navigational path information: posts arrived at, e.g., via related or promoted links from another post are implicitly noting the value of both that link and target content.

Explicit and implicit curation actions are recorded and can be weighted and used to present contextually appropriate content and functionality to creators, editors and curators throughout the community. Curation can also include selecting content for additional promotion—giving a story a position on the home page, e.g.

Curation tools include (1) recommending a post or comment, (2) selecting content for inclusion on the home or a section index page and (3) selecting content for other packaging including Editor's Picks, special feeds or newsletters. Curation tools are contextual. They are presented to members according to the scope of their role and per any pre-existing content categorization.

Use Case 3: Editor

A member with the role of Technology Editor is permitted to categorize new content as *Technology*. Within the Technology section, that Editor can promote a story to appear on the home page or above the fold on the section index page by noting it as an Editor's Pick (Fig. 2.3).

While writing a new article, opportunities to see relevant keywords, archival content, and trending topics are presented. This can be in a sidebar, an overlay or via contextual-click.

2 Empowering the Distributed Editorial Workforce   17

Fig. 2.3: Assigning a post to the Technology section

Use Case 4: Creator

Within the course of writing a paragraph, suggested links to related images and news sources appear in the sidebar of the editing tool. Via an explicit request, creators can reach out to Aardvark (http://vark.com), LinkedIn Answers (http://www.linkedin.com/answers), or a specific Twitter (http://twitter.com) list or tag for verification or amplification of their topic-in-progress (see Figs. 2.4 and 2.5).

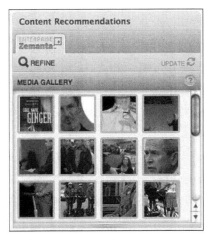
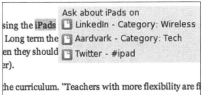

Fig. 2.4: Recommendation of related images   Fig. 2.5: Request of further information for a term

Reaching out to the community with "Here's what I know. Here's what I don't know. What do you know?" [3] helps accomplish more work and involves the community more deeply in the process. This deepens sense of community—it is a virtuous cycle of increasing engagement.

Once the new content is published, a list of community members who are active commentators or curators of similar content can be presented to creators. The opportunity to promote relevant content to the relevant people—presuming community members have given permission [2]—presents creators with the ability to find a community and helps the community find relevant content.

Based on what the creator or editor is working on, she may want more contextual information or may wish that contextual information to be even less intrusive. Creators have options for contextual presentation to best fit their work-styles.

The data are available as are the tools to get at and present it. The challenge is to present such data and information to the creator as organically as possible, to present related information naturally so that it is easily discoverable and utilized, but not so it overtly interrupts the creator's workflow.

2.3 Roles, Rights and Reputation

When building a CMS to serve a growing network of writers, editors and participants, *Who are you? What are you allowed to do here? What have you done previously?* are core to execution from business and technology points of view. Roles and Rights cover who you are and what you are permitted to do within the system. Reputation refers to the credibility and trust built up through historical activities and is the measure by which participants can be promoted through the system by gaining authorization to perform additional editorial tasks.

2.3.1 Definition of Role

A role is a defined list of tasks a community member is authorized to perform. Roles create a replicable model for adding new talent to the team. The team includes salaried staffers and others who are compensated via stipends, performance bonuses and other monetary and non-monetary rewards. Defining roles for participants provides the framework for creating a highly scalable distributed workforce. This scalability can include a one-person operation looking to recruit and manage wider community participation to large organizations looking to augment their editorial staff.

Everyone who visits and participates in the content created via the CMS is a member of the community. All roles are included under *Community Members*; they are differentiated by their authorization levels—in the degree to which they can interact with the content.

Reputation also provides a path for advancement through the system and incentives to work toward this advancement. These incentives are designed to drive deeper engagement and to advance the goals of the publisher as well as the community as a whole [5].

2.3.2 Basic Roles and Rights

1. Creator: Somebody who can publish and manage their own content
2. Editor: Somebody who can publish and manage content as well as manage others' content
3. Curator: Someone who can, explicitly or implicitly, note content as worthwhile
4. Community Member: anyone interacting with content on the platform

Being able to slot people into these defined roles allows for the scaling of a distributed workforce into the thousands. Measuring the performance of individuals in these roles means we can modify responsibilities based on individuals' actions. Reputation is a key component of managing these individuals in their roles; Reputation will be explored in detail in the following paragraph. Focus on community member-recruitment is based on collective needs and interests.

2.3.3 Reputation

Reputation is the history of a creator, piece of content or community member. Reputation's purpose is to make default decisions about quality based on historical activities (cf. [1]). Reputation will help inform re the best creators, editors, curators, community members and content. In this sense, *best* is not particularly subjective: Reputation is an amalgam of desirable behaviours and formulated weightings and scores based on these. Reputation can drive compensation. Reputation can be employed as a first-line filter: when there is a lot of content for editors to consume and process, sorting by reputation can provide an efficient first step.

The primary usage of Reputation is as an initial filtration system: content and community input can be sorted by and presented to editors by reputation order. Using these weightings, we will be able to present various tangible benefits or capabilities to those we have weighted. Another purpose is to drive participation in desirable behaviours throughout the system via rewards.

Desirable behaviours include actions like writing posts, leaving comments and generating page views. Participation in desirable behaviours will drive tangible benefits, e.g.:

- Creators with better reputations may have their content promoted more frequently
- Community members with higher reputation scores may have their comments displayed ahead of comments with members with lower reputation scores
- Content with better reputation may be promoted in more places; Content with better reputation may be displayed ahead of content with lesser reputation

Participation in these behaviours informs numeric weightings for each creator, each community member and each piece of content in the system. Reputation quotient is a score kept of an amalgam of desired behaviours, actions and occurrences.

Examples for reputation quotients for creators, community members and content are given in the following:

- Reputation quotient for a creator, e.g., includes how frequently that creator logs in, posts and comments on others' articles.
- Reputation quotient for content includes page views and comments received, referrals and quality of referral sources. These same positively affect the creator of that content.
- Reputation quotient for community members includes logins, comments left, comments up-voted and replied-to by others and curation actions completed.

A community member who has participated in enough desirable behaviours that they have achieved a high reputation score would have their subsequent comments, e.g., default to a higher score. A highly reputed community member could be made known to the creator(s) she follows.

Another tangible benefit for a creator or editor could be enabling them to curate the home page based on having reached a threshold through desirable behaviours.

In all, a reputation system helps keep management informed as the value grows across the network. It is also a tireless watcher of cross-network activity: 24 x 7 x 365.25, it is seeing and remembering all desirable behaviours performed. This combination of automation and human intelligence allows us to build a network of creators, community members and content with definable credentials. It gives us actionable insight into the relative value of our participants. The system will be extensible as to what can inform it—new metrics and desired behaviours—and what it informs—new roles and capabilities for those meeting thresholds.

It is designed do all this with minimal manual intervention: as we envision new roles – deputies, acolytes, network programmers for a day – we can create workflows that enable them automatically with reputation as the core of a self-healing, spontaneously-creative system than can help us scale our network and business.

Use Case 5: Editor

> The Technology Editor logs in to update section home page. There have been 30 new posts and 90 new comments since she logged in last. Presenting her with posts from creators and community members with the highest reputation quotients first is one way to prioritize which content she should promote and use to refresh the Technology section home page (Fig. 2.6).

Arming intelligent and engaged community members—including staffers and the more distributed workforce—allows content management decisions to be made based on science *and* art. That community members, staffers and the wider team also have reputation scores associated with them means their actions and behaviours can be measured and managed: Publishers can ensure needs are being met to the mutual

2 Empowering the Distributed Editorial Workforce 21

Fig. 2.6: Prioritisation of posts

benefit of all; Editors can spend their limited resources first on the most highly-reputed content; Members of the community can decide to read and engage with most highly reputed content and creators. All members are provided incentive to engage more deeply with content throughout the system.

A lingua franca for reputation—a standard protocol that captures desired behaviours—would enable the portability of reputation across CMSs, sites and communities. There has been work to create a standard activity stream protocol (http://activitystrea.ms); that protocol could be extended to provide scores and weightings against those activities. Diaspora (http://www.joindiaspora.com) and the DiSo (http://diso-project.org) projects both have goals of distributed, portable activities and reputation. Additional sites could use those concepts, add their own desired behaviours, and authorize community members within their own CMSs accordingly.

2.4 Conclusion

Much of this CMS work is available for implementation today. The pieces around creation, roles, rights, reputation and the semantic tools certainly exist and can be improved upon and integrated to suit individual organizations' needs. Execution comes to definition, adoption, customization and usage.

For more traditional organizations, especially, there is a learning curve: less-formal editorial workflows — as there is where creators have less direct editorial oversight and there is little to no direct approval process -— necessitate a ceding of direct control of the messaging. Publishers, Public Relations, Corporate Communications, and Marketing departments are used to strong, direct control. Trust in, and monitoring of, how the wider community manages content quality has to be learned through experience. But the benefits of distributed editorial systems should be clear: the ability to massively distribute workload and the creation of ecosystems that are mutually beneficial to publishers, creators, editors, and community members.

References

1. Farmer, R., Glass, B.: Building Web Reputation Systems, 1st edn. O'Reilly, Sebastopol, CA, USA (2010)
2. Godin, S.: Music lessons (2008). URL http://sethgodin.typepad.com/seths_blog/2008/01/music-lessons.html
3. Jarvis, J.: Denton goes to the bench (2007). URL http://www.buzzmachine.com/2007/12/14/denton-goes-to-the-bench/
4. Rosen, J.: The people formerly known as the audience (2006). URL http://archive.pressthink.org/2006/06/27/ppl_frmr.html
5. Yahoo Developer Network: Reputation (2010). URL http://developer.yahoo.com/ypatterns/social/people/reputation/index.html

Biographical Notes

Steve McNally creates platforms and processes to empower the distributed editorial workforce at Forbes Media. Previously, Steve oversaw technology architecture, software development and site operations as CTO for True/Slant (which Forbes acquired in June 2010). He came to True/Slant from Condé Nast, where he spent eight years, most recently as Senior Director, Product Development. In that role he managed the build-out of Parade.com's core publishing platform. Prior to that, Steve managed channel development for About.com, where he designed, built and launched an affiliate ad network. Steve also worked for Prodigy Internet and IBM where he built knowledge management, business intelligence, communication and collaboration tools for internal teams and partners.

Chapter 3
The Rise of Semantic-aware Applications

Stéphane Croisier

Abstract Last decade was focused on building up semantic foundations required to turn the semantic utopia into reality. The adoption of those technologies is now happening rapidly and we should support the development of a new generation of semantically enriched applications. The technical conditions are excellent. Today, the Deep Web is ubiquitous. Structured and unstructured data are available in quantities never seen before. Growth perspectives are exponential. And we all start to be impacted by a tsunami of information in our daily life. Information overload, the lack of proper filters and the absence of smart content are becoming real problems. Accordingly, users expect to see the arrival of new concrete and effective solutions now. Semantic technologies are available that may overcome those problems but no one found the semantic killer application yet. In this contribution, we discuss some of the latest semantic challenges and the future of content management systems.

3.1 Introduction

Information growth is accelerating at a phenomenal rate due to emails, shared network drives, Content Management Systems (CMSs), information databases, social networks or the global web, coupled to a massive cost reduction in physical storage and the democratization of tools that favour content creation and data capture. Information Systems and the Web in general met their expectations: they became widely used commodities able to link hundreds of millions of users and billions of content items. As a result, there is a vast number of content and information available. This avalanche of mainly unstructured data is not only starting to impact and to drown top executives but it influences every one of us, both as consumers or as information workers. Information overload and the lack of adequate contextual filtering

---

Stéphane Croisier
Co-Founder and Strategic Product Advisor, Jahia Solutions Group SA, Switzerland, e-mail: scroisier@jahia.com

mechanisms, the ever-ending multiplication of non-compliant and non-connected information silos and the limit of search engines based on simple keyword queries that generate flat result lists are beginning to considerably hurt our efficiency and productivity.

As time goes by, such problems will continue to impact our daily life, too. And problems are generally a big call to creative and innovative solutions. Mallela from Kosmix stated recently: "We are in the midst of another revolutionary transformation as the web morphs itself into a richer collection of services, APIs and apps along with text and links. Along the way the web is getting smarter about what it holds. Call it semantic web or Deep Web or Web 3.0 or any other term you want to call it but the transformation is real ... albeit slow" [2].

How can we better tap into this ocean of unstructured information available on the public Web or behind the companies' closed garden walls? How can we help users automatically discover the needle in the haystack wherever the information lives? And more importantly: how can we deliver a new range of contextual and semantic applications, which could bring the customized solutions that are needed to solve each of these information problems in a personalized way? To rapidly and effectively develop and build such content-rich sites and applications, developers and end-users need now to have access to a new generation of tools and features: This is the goal of semantic-aware CMSs. Next, we discuss four challenges of semantic-aware applications and the future of CMSs.

3.2 First Challenge: Easing the Connections with Smart and Trusted Information Warehouses

The vision of the semantic web is that it might be able to eventually help people solve very difficult problems by using connections between apparently unrelated concepts. Meant are connections that would take many people many years to perceive, but they could become obvious through kinds of associations made possible by semantic-aware applications. Accordingly, Nova Spivack wrote a few years ago: "Although the intelligence of the Web is not very evident at first glance, nonetheless it can be found if you look for it. This intelligence doesn't exist across the entire Web yet, it only exists in islands that are few and far between compared to the vast amount of information on the Web as a whole. But these islands are growing, and more are appearing every year, and they are starting to connect together. And as this happens the collective intelligence of the Web is increasing." [3]. The underlying statement of Spivack is what I call Smart and Trusted Information Warehouses. From Wikipedia (http://www.wikipedia.org) to Freebase (http://www.freebase.com) and the Internet Movie Database (http://www.imdb.com), we contribute to a new generation of Information Hubs that all start to become accessible through easy to use programmatic services and which give access to their smart, curated and trusted content sources. These Information Hubs are radically changing the way we develop new applications. Suddenly, we start to figure out that we could develop a new range of applications which could syndicate, reuse, combine and mash-up several of those remote services into larger works rather than having to develop yet another new disconnected and proprietary content application.

Even though not all of these content-rich services are semantic web ready from a technical perspective, their consequences are quite similar: stop thinking in terms of silos and start connecting the dots together. That is, the Deep Web is already becoming more intelligent and even without Semantic Web technologies. And this trend becomes the starting point of a new generation of more-heavily interconnected services and applications.

Various industries become more and more aware of the importance of linking data and services all together. This was recently the case for the public administration sector with the multiplication of *Gov 2.0* initiatives leading to an increased consciousness to open some data. Automatically a new generation of companies such as Factiva (http://www.factiva.com) or Socrata (http://www.socrata.com) emerge to better syndicate and provide additional value added services on top of this new *collective intelligence*. On the other end of the value chain, this starts to have a direct impact on the way private companies envision Enterprise Software until now. Enterprise Content and Enterprise Applications can be easily enriched with such public, trusted and smart information sources. Boundaries between the public and the private web are fading out. From an end-user perspective, employees begin to ask for access to some Wikipedia definitions or to such public administration data straight from within their context of use and directly within their enterprise-grade applications.

The raise of these information warehouses will definitively bring forward a new generation of tools and utilities at the convergence between Portal, Search and Semantic Publishing (cf. Fig. 3.1). Such crossover applications will be built around improved content syndication, data federation, easy mashing up, text enrichment and document repurposing coming from all these trusted information sources and will repurpose them into new personalized and compelling user experiences.

3.3 Second Challenge: Automating the Semantic Geekery

The second challenge is not only to facilitate the connections with these islands of well-established, structured, standardized and trusted information sources but to be able to leverage the rest of the unstructured information which lies around us in different systems.

There are two approaches to develop the semantic capacity of information systems. First, the bottom-up approach is problematic as it assumes metadata will be added to each piece of content to include additional information about its context. This approach will mainly work for the top-notch information warehouses mentioned above. Second, the top-down approach might have more success for the rest of the data, as it focuses on developing automated natural language-based text annotation capabilities. In contrast to the bottom-up approach, those annotation capabil-

Fig. 3.1: Qwiki: A new way to dynamically compose a new user experience by mashing up together various trusted information sources.

ities can make similar kinds of determinations possible without adding any special metadata and without requiring any additional extra-work.

The notion of Content Intelligence is limited too often to a restricted set of semantic web technologies such as RDF, OWL and SPARQL. It is important to extend this scope to a whole new generation of content analysis tools and frameworks that allow meaning to be automatically inferred from content and context. Seth Grimes, a well-known expert in the field, defines smart content as "the product of content analytics, enriched with semantic meaning, as the adaptation of BI techniques and processes to unstructured online, social, and enterprise sources" [1]. Even if some of those tools are still under development and errors and incorrectly identified bits of content are not unusual, we can expect to see significant progresses in the next years.

However, commoditization of such kind of services are increasingly available today and various automated content enrichment and annotation applications such as OpenCalais (http://www.opencalais.com), Evri (http://www.evri.com), Saplo (http://www.saplo.com), Zemanta (http://www.zemanta.com, cf. Fig. 3.2), AlchemyAPI (http://www.alchemyapi.com) or SalsaDev (http://www.salsadev.com) are in the cloud and promise to automatically inject added values to your raw content. As 90 per cent of the content is still totally unstructured, or at best tagged and categorized but archived and isolated into their own content silo and classification schema, we should contribute to the fast rise of automated text analysis tools. These tools could tap into the large mass of unstructured information and automatically unveil its semantic richness. Today, automated text analysis services automatically extract additional information and can be categorized into two groups:

- **Content Enrichments Services** provide keyword suggestions, topic and entity extraction, sentiment analysis and other forms of automated classification performed at a text or document.
- **Content Relationships Services** match and discover hidden relationships between text paragraphs with similar meaning. They further link raw content with other trusted linked data or information sources.

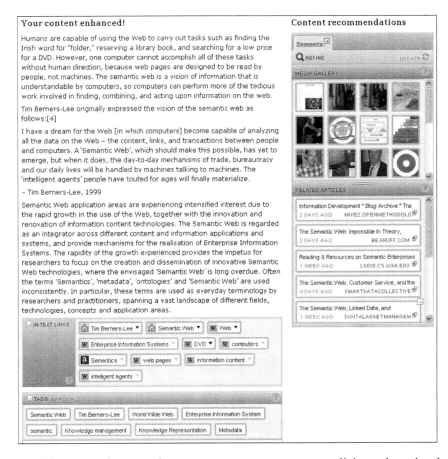

Fig. 3.2: Automatic suggestions to annotate your content or to link to other related information sources while editing your content with Zemanta

However, enriching content and adding smarter content relationships is only one step towards better-personalized and contextualized applications. The second challenge with regard to this new generation of *smart content* players is to automate the provisioning of the right information at the right person not only based on the meaning of raw text paragraphs but also inferred from the context of use. Relevance is relative. It is first and foremost about the intent of a user. Contextual content prediction—at the crossroads between content and user analytics—is the next *Holy Grail* that can finally add this new layer of intelligent filtering and contextualized content delivery we are all expecting. The next challenge is then to learn and infer behaviours to automatically predict your reading interests, consumption taste, the next actions to take or even extrapolate on how the future will look like (cf. Fig. 3.3).

Tackling such a challenge to automatically curate content according to your consumption behaviours and to surface the best will require a winning combination of several key emerging technologies such as:

- Semantic-readiness to automatically understand the meaning of content
- Schema-free utilities to leverage and tap into heterogeneous information sources
- Context-awareness combined to strong user analytics and machine-learning algorithms to get personal preferences

During the last decade companies like Cognos[1] or Business Objects[2] built success stories by providing the tools to better exploit and leverage Data Intelligence. We should now contribute to the rise of Content Intelligence and Content Analytical solutions that automatically transform raw content into relevant findings.

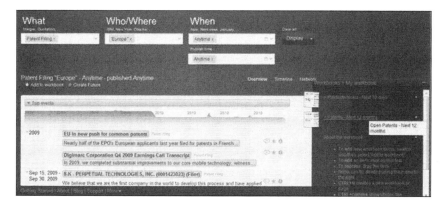

Fig. 3.3: Recorded Future (http://www.recordedfuture.com): Prediction Software based on the next generation of Content Intelligence tools and algorithms

---

[1] http://www-01.ibm.com/software/data/cognos/

[2] http://www.sap.com/solutions/sapbusinessobjects/index.epx

3.4 Third Challenge: Delivering Compelling Information Experiences

Bridging the gap between specialized semantic gurus and content consumers is the third challenge of the semantic industry. Semantic techniques, algorithms and standards take precedence over real user needs. Andraz Tori (CTO of Zemanta) argues in a tough-provoking presentation: "We need to tailor the experience to specific use-cases, ignoring (powerful) technology at first and spending more than 10% of the time figuring out where the software/data are going to be used in practice. User experience is not just graphics design" [4].

Indeed, we should try to effectively solve concrete information problems throughout the integration of semantic tools in combination to new pervasive ways to experience information access and discovery. The use of semantic technologies should become much more immersive than it is now whereby they are transparently integrated into the usage context (cf. Fig. 3.4).

The semantic industry can learn a lot from eCommerce. Online shops helped consumers explore and discover products by focusing first on the user experience. By telling consumers which products are available by dynamic classification, faceted navigation, purchase recommendations, spotlighting results, online shops supported them to find the needle in the haystack. Similarly, the search industry is also trying to reinvent itself through the integration of improved user experiences. As stated by Stefan Weitz (Director Microsoft Bing) "the ability for an engine to do more than return a bunch of links that put the burden of exploration on the human is a model that needs a refresh. Determining intent of the query—through explicit or implicit means—and trying to build an experience (whether its through brokered apps or pre-processed info) that helps people navigate the new online landscape—that is where we need to be headed" [5].

Enriching the user information experience within its usage context is then rapidly becoming a critical piece of the puzzle that was too often neglected in favour of more technical challenges, to finally get massive adoption of new semantic capabilities.

3.5 Future of CMS: Fostering Rapid Development and Assembly of Semantic-aware Applications

All these trustful information islands surrounded by an ocean of content automatically enriched, mashed up and cross-referenced are, however, nothing without the capability to develop rapidly semantic-aware applications that are able to successfully leverage and turn all these additional metadata and links into concrete, business-solving applications. The promise of these semantic-aware applications is to help us see connections that exist but that are invisible to current CMSs.

Semantic-aware applications evolved from Search Based Applications (SBA). According to Wikipedia, SBAs are "software applications in which a search en-

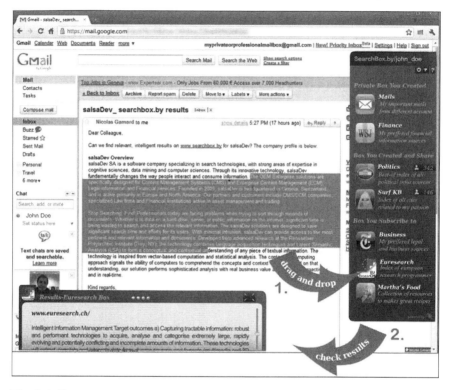

Fig. 3.4: Context-aware, socially-curated and semantically-empowered information experience by SalsaDev's new SearchBox line of product.

gine platform is used as the core infrastructure for information access and reporting. SBAs use semantic technologies to aggregate, normalize and classify unstructured, semi-structured and/or structured content across multiple repositories, and employ natural language technologies for accessing the aggregated information." [3] This should open the doors to new ways of contextually accessing and consuming relevant information wherever they live (cf. 3.5).

The next generation of CMSs will commoditize the way developers and power end-users can rapidly design, assemble and compose such applications, at a lower price, through point and click interfaces, without having to necessarily understand the whole technical complexity required to generate such semantic-aware sites or applications.

Such systems will become the new visual designer of the Semantic Web, in which you will be able to create standard, open, content-rich, social ready and semantic-aware applications, boosting developers and end-users productivity without compromising flexibility. It should help eliminate the complexity of developing common 3.0 sites and applications, leveraging both local or external information warehouses,

---

[3] http://en.wikipedia.org/wiki/Search-based_application, retrieved November 29, 2010

automatically enriching unstructured content, and providing the tools needed to rapidly create, assemble and compose contextual and semantic-aware applications (cf. Fig. 3.6).

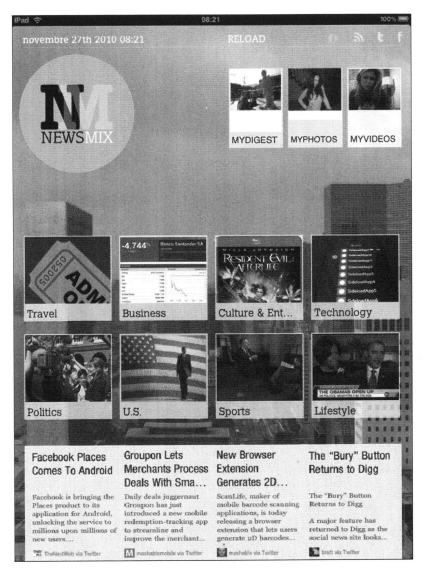

Fig. 3.5: Sobees NewsMix (http://www.sobees.com), a semantic-aware application which automatically curate social media articles, surface the best and repurpose them into a compelling magazine-like format.

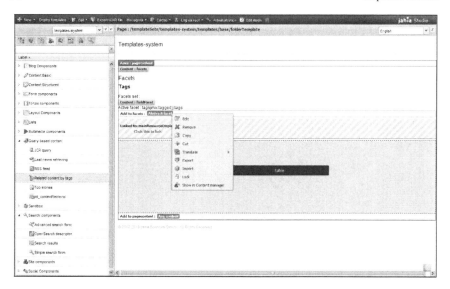

Fig. 3.6: Jahia Studio: Rapid Visual Assembly of Semantic-Aware Applications

3.6 Conclusion

Semantic technologies are bringing today the core foundation to better understand and exploit the rich volume of information available out there. The challenges of this decade will be now to build effective solutions on this new infrastructure. The Semantic Web is mostly a data interchange layer aimed at application developers. Semantic-aware applications and tools behind must become much more intuitive than they are today hiding complexity and favouring more immersive and contextualized user experiences. There are hundreds of business problems we can solve with today's technology without having to wait for a smarter future. The current limit is primarily based on one's imagination and on bringing a new layer of semantic simplicity to end-users. Providing and working on a compelling information experience will be incredibly beneficial. If one starts any new semantic project by thinking first about user experience, then magic things will occur.

References

1. Grimes, S.: This is content intelligence (2010). URL http://www.cmswire.com/cms/information-management/this-is-content-intelligence-according-to-4-experts-008811.php
2. Mallela, M.: Can apple reinvent the meaning of 'search'? (2010). URL http://blog.kosmix.com/?p=1262
3. Spivack, N.: Minding the planet: The meaning and future of the semantic web (without publication date). URL http://lifeboat.com/ex/minding.the.planet

4. Tori, A.: Semantic web user interface – do they have to be ugly? (2010). URL http://www.slideshare.net/andraz/semtech2010-do-semanticwebuserinterfaceshavetobeugly
5. Weitz, S.: Comment on 'John battelle on the future of search' post by g. hotchkiss (2010). URL http://searchengineland.com/john-battelle-on-the-future-of-search-38382#comment-9255

Biographical Notes

Stéphane is one of the Co-Founder of Jahia Solutions Group (www.jahia.com), a Java-based Open Source Web Content Management Solution which integrates a CMS, a Portal Server and some Document Management and Social capabilities into the same product offering. He's active in the Content Management Industry back from the nineties. He currently acts as an executive in residence, advisor and board member in various content and semantically rich initiatives including the IKS project. Beside Jahia, he maintains relations with SalsaDev and Sobees, two other companies mentioned in this article. You can follow Stéphane on Twitter (@scroisier) or on his personal blog (http://scroisier.posterous.com/).

Chapter 4
Simplified Semantic Enhancement of JCR-based Content Applications

Bertrand Delacretaz and Michael Marth

Abstract Traditional content management systems (CMS) usually do not understand the meaning of the content that they manage. Enabling that understanding through semantic tools could allow CMS developers and users to work more efficiently. However, this often requires a whole new set of tools and skills. As heavy users and spec lead of JCR, the industry standard Java Content Repository API, we view this semantic technology from a pragmatic angle and tried to find a way to introduce it in a soft way, with minimal changes and very little added complexity. Our plan as presented in this chapter is to store simple semi-structured semantic annotations alongside with our content. Storing annotations in a JCR-friendly way allows us to use standard JCR query tools to discover and link content items based on semantic metadata. This will provide added value to developers working with our products, in a simple and non-disruptive way.

4.1 Introduction

This chapter starts by a description of a number of use cases that require semantic metadata and add value to our existing CMS offering. We then present the JCR[1] content storage model, and explain how we intend to store semantic annotations in simplified form to make them searchable with JCR. We also discuss the software components that need to be added to our CMS to enable this simple yet effective

---

Bertrand Delacretaz
Senior R&D developer, Day Software (now part of Adobe), Switzerland, e-mail: bdelacre@adobe.com

Michael Marth
Technical Evangelist, Day Software (now part of Adobe), Switzerland, e-mail: mmarth@adobe.com

[1] JCR is the Java Content Repository API, JSR-283, http://jcp.org/en/jsr/detail?id=283, and our products use its reference implementation which is Jackrabbit, http://jackrabbit.apache.org

semantic enhancement, and finally evaluate the risks, benefits and drawbacks of this approach. Even though a lot of this is specific to JCR, the general principles can be adapted to many different types of CMS.

4.2 Use Cases for Semantic Content Enhancement and Search

We now discuss a number of use cases where semantic metadata adds value to our products. We will assume that a semantic engine is available which provides the required functionality to help us improve our CMS.

4.2.1 Core Language Help for Content Authors

A major goal of CMS is to support authors during the content creation process. Let us consider some possible benefits of a CMS that understands content and assists authors accordingly. Most CMS offer a spell checker at authoring time. Language detection, however, is implemented much less often. Imagine a CMS that figures out in which language an author is currently writing: the CMS can set a property on the content, so that rendering templates know which language the template should use, all without intervention of an author.

Analysing text can go much further. Large corporate web sites often have style guides for the language that can be used on their web site. For example, a guiding rule could be that colloquial terms or slang are to be avoided. The CMS can support authors by either warning them when they deviate from predefined guidelines or by highlighting content whose style significantly differs from other content's language style.

4.2.2 Putting Content in the Context of Other Content Items

A semantic CMS can also help authors put new content in context with existing content. While new content is created the CMS can search existing content for similar or related items. In the user interface of a large intranet or wiki where often no author has a complete overview of the content, the CMS can bring up a list of similar pages to prevent the author from re-creating existing content. The author can also use a CMS-supplied list of related pages that might be useful for site visitors, and link some of them to the new content.

Tagging content is another repetitive task where a semantic CMS can help authors. Once the CMS is aware of enough similar content it can suggest tags to the author, who only needs to select them from a list rather than having to think about which tags to create. A nice side effect is improving the consistency of tags in the whole content.

As a third application, content similarity search can be used to reduce the number of different tags in an existing content repository. Consider a CMS where authors have tagged content with, for instance, *football*, *foot ball* and *soccer*. A semantic CMS can notice that these tags share the same meaning, and suggest combining them.

Finally, in many content repositories certain pages act as reference pages for specific topics. An airline web site can have a page about the A380 plane that always gets linked to whenever the A380 is mentioned in the content. Again, repetitive authorial tasks can be reduced if the CMS extracts such rules and offers authors to automatically create those links.

4.2.3 Putting Content in the Context of the Real World

Automatically recognizing entities and offering them to authors can be beneficial for setting external links, too. A CMS, for instance, can recognize street addresses in a text paragraph and could offer them to create links to the corresponding Google Maps URL. Similarly, entities like well-known people or locations can be recognized and corresponding links can be suggested to the author. The fragment *Barack Obama*, for example could prompt the CMS to offer links to the White House's web site and to Mr. Obama's Wikipedia page.

4.2.4 User-generated Content

User-generated content (UGC) is all the rage since the start of the Web 2.0 hype. Today, hardly any new web site can do without user-generated ratings, comments or similar content.

Even moderate amounts of UGC, like user comments, can result in significant operative maintenance efforts. Spam comments need to be removed, for example, and their quantities can grow a lot at times, out of the control of the site authors. This is where semantic technologies can help, by automatically marking suspicious comments as spam. Analysis of sentiments in comments or forum posts can also help prioritize forum moderation queues, for example, to make sure very negative posts get immediate attention.

4.2.5 Semantic Image Similarity

This use case was initially published on our blog [1]. We include it here as an important example of semantic enhancements that do not require any new skills from the CMS user, yet can bring a lot of added value.

Figure 4.1 shows a picture taken on a trip to Iceland a few years ago. A typical Icelandic house with a typical big Icelandic four-wheel drive vehicle parked in front and a canoe on top. The childish drawing in Fig. 4.2 has much the same content, at the semantic level: a big car in front of a house, with a boat on top of the car. It is not too stylish, but the same basic information is in there. Including a smiling sun of course, which you might get in Iceland every ten minutes in between showers.

Fig. 4.1: Typical Icelandic scene   Fig. 4.2: Young Bertrand's drawing

Humans immediately identify both images as describing a similar scene. Getting your CMS to recognize this similarity, however, is another matter. You need a good *semantic* understanding of the images to find out that they pretty much tell the same story. It is not just about the raw bits.

Assuming the required semantic image analysis tools are available, can we graft such an image similarity detection feature to our existing JCR-based CMS? We will try to answer that question later in this chapter.

4.2.6 The Semantic Engine as an Assistant – Not a Master

In all the use cases shown above, semantic metadata and the related matching and search algorithms can add a lot of value to the content creation process, almost without requiring authors to learn anything new. Like a good human assistant, the semantic engine should know when to make suggestions and when to stay out of the way, to avoid overwhelming its *boss* with useless information and chatter.

For us, this also means not overwhelming CMS developers with lots of new concepts and tools, as much as possible. Using Furtwangen IKS Semantic Engine (FISE) [2] for content enhancement, and designing a simplified storage and query model that represents just a few additions to what we currently use in our products, will help those developers make a smooth transition to semantically-enriched content.

4.3 Missing Pieces

This section presents a short description of the software components that we need to add to our out-of-the box JCR-based CMS setup to implement the use cases described above.

4.3.1 Content Enhancement Engine

The FISE content enhancement engine can be used to add semantic annotations to our content. Sending a piece of text that contains *Barack Obama* to it, for example, will return an annotation pointing to a semantic entity of type Person, with a link to Mr. Obama's Wikipedia page, and a connected entity of type *Organization* which refers to the White House.

The RESTful interface of FISE makes it easy to integrate it with our CMS: sending an HTTP POST request to FISE will cause its configured content enhancement engines to process the text supplied in the request, and return annotations in RDF format.

As we write this, FISE does not provide the entity detection engine for images that we need to implement our semantic image similarity use case. However, integrating such an engine in FISE is easy once the necessary algorithms are available. The idea of FISE is to serve as an orchestration framework to host multiple such enhancement engines, routing incoming requests to them, combining results and providing a simple front-end for content enhancement. Researchers working on semantic annotation algorithms can easily plug them in to FISE, making them available to CMS developers with no or few changes on the CMS integration side.

In time, once the required enhancement engines are available, FISE should fulfill all content enhancement requirements for our use cases. Currently only text-based use cases can be covered, and the quality of the enhancements probably needs some tuning, but we can already start integrating FISE into our products, to demonstrate those features and integrate the corresponding user interface elements in our system.

4.3.2 Semantic Metadata Storage

RDF annotations returned by FISE could be stored as is in a semantic triple store, most of which also provide semantic queries (usually SPARQL-based) out of the box.

However, we are not enthusiastic about adding a different storage component to our system. The beauty of JCR is that it stores a wide variety of content natively: structured database-like metadata, unstructured or semi-structured pieces of content and large binary files. Adding a secondary storage for our semantic triples would complicate the life of our CMS administrators, introduce a number of new possible failure points and in general make our product more complicated than what we really need to implement our use cases.

To avoid this additional complexity, and assuming we do not need the full power of arbitrary semantic storage and querying, we have been looking for a way of storing the semantic metadata in simplified form, consistent with our usual way of working with JCR, and without exposing more semantic technology than what is strictly needed to implement our use cases.

Although we will store the semantic metadata in a simplified form, we want to avoid losing any information, to be able to consider additional semantic information later, if we realize that we have ignored too much of what FISE provides.

4.3.3 Semantic Queries

Several of our use cases require querying semantic annotations provided by FISE. Like for the storage part, we want to avoid adding more critical or complex new components to our system than we strictly need. Storing semantic information in a way that is friendly to JCR queries as they are implemented today will help us avoid that additional complexity. This introduces some limitations on the types of queries that we can run, so we will need to check that our use cases are covered.

4.3.4 User Interfaces

Some user interface enhancements will be needed, mostly to suggest semantic annotations, links and other metadata at the content authoring stage. Discussing this is out of the scope of this chapter; we will concentrate on the server-side machinery that enables our use cases. See Steve McNally's chapter for a discussion of user interfaces.

4.4 JCR-Based Implementation

A warning is required here: we have not implemented the above use cases yet. What follows is an initial design, based on informal experiments, that we believe will enable them with minimal disruption to our existing system. This is a first approach that will need to be refined once we are able to test it at scale.

4.4.1 JCR Storage Model: Nodes, Properties and Node Types

The storage model of a JCR content repository is a (potentially big) tree of *nodes* and *properties*. Nodes are used to organize the tree, starting with a single root node as in a Unix file system. Each node has a unique path that starts with a single slash for the root node. For example, the following path for a page */content/iksbook/authors* describes the authors of this book.

A JCR node can have an arbitrary number of properties, which can be of different data types: strings, numbers, boolean values, binary streams that can store multimedia content, etc. Our */content/iksbook/authors* page, for example, could have a property named *text* that stores the textual content of the page.

JCR node types can be used to set constraints on sub nodes and properties. They are defined in a simple description language similar in functionality to a database or XML schema, and each node has a primary node type that points to such a definition. Node type definitions enable the full spectrum of constraints, from completely unstructured content to rigid database-like structures. We don't use lots of constraints in our products, according to the wisdom of David's Model [3] that fosters agility in development and evolution of content. David's model recommends starting with the *nt:unstructured* node type, a built-in definition that sets no constraints to allow fully unstructured content. We believe in a *content* first approach in our systems, and as such almost always start with *nt:unstructured*, and add constraints only where strictly needed.

4.4.2 JCR Micro-trees and Content Trees

As we have seen, the JCR storage model is a fairly simple one, but JCR beginners often wonder about how to structure their content, and what its granularity should be. Does a JCR node map to a full page of content, just one paragraph, one run of text in a given style, or something else?

The key is to view the JCR tree as a hierarchy of micro-trees, each with their own structural rules or conventions that are combined to form a larger macro-structure. In our products, the main unit of content is a page micro-tree, which contains a paragraph system micro-tree that, in turn, contains the various content elements that form a page.

A website page will usually consist of a number of these JCR-level pages: one for the main content, one for a marketing campaign block in a corner of the webpage, a sub-page for the comments in a blog post, etc. For us, a JCR-level page is a group of content items that belong together. Figure 4.3 depicts a typical JCR micro-tree for such a page.

The organization of that micro-tree is simple to understand, based on the tree structure and node names. The page name is *banking*, and its main sub tree is rooted at the *par* node, which is what we call a paragraph system: a container for other micro-trees that build the page content: text blocks, images, structural elements like column breaks, etc.

Besides this *par* sub node, the *jcr:content* node of our page contains a few other nodes for additional content elements: the main title, the main image, etc. When the corresponding website or mobile page is built for publication, those micro-trees are aggregated as needed to create the final published content. At a higher level, those page micro-trees are combined to form the macro-tree that organizes our CMS pages, as shown in Fig. 4.4 below.

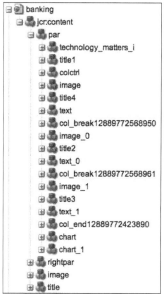

Fig. 4.3: JCR page micro-tree   Fig. 4.4: JCR content macro-tree

This macro-tree reflects the author's view of the content, a view that makes sense at the organizational level, where */content/iks/marketing*, for example, could be the marketing content of the IKS website. In this case, our website *geometrixx*—that is the name of a fictitious company that we use for examples in our products—contains a number of versions in different languages. The English version contains sections like products, services or events and are arranged in a straightforward structure that corresponds to the website structure and URLs. We do not use fancy mappings of website URLs to content paths in our products if we can avoid it, as a one-to-one mapping is much simpler to understand and requires no configuration.

This micro / macro tree view gives a lot of flexibility in defining and evolving content structures, while making things easy to understand at all levels if node names are chosen carefully. As we will see next, this flexibility allows us to add our semantic metadata to the page content without reconfiguring anything, as the constraints on the page sub tree are loose enough to allow for new nodes that were not planned in our current content structure.

4.4.3 Semantic Metadata in Micro-trees

As the node type definition of our page nodes allows it, we can store our semantic metadata as a micro-tree under the page node, more precisely, under the *jcr:content* sub node that we use by convention for all page content. In the example depicted in Fig. 4.5 we have added an *annotations* sub node under the *jcr:content* node, assuming FISE provided the following annotations:

- Person: Barack Obama
- Organization: White House
- Place: Washington DC
- Related: http://www.whitehouse.gov
- Related: http://en.wikipedia.org/wiki/Barack_Obama

This is already a simplified notation: the RDF data returned by FISE would say that our piece of content is related to those entities, and it would use precise semantic namespaces and URIs to identify the entity types *Person* and identities *Barack Obama*.

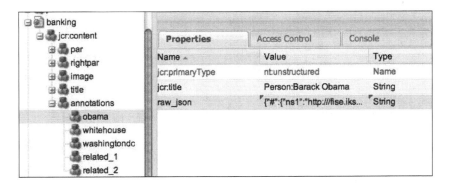

Fig. 4.5: semantic annotations in page micro-tree

This simplified notation not only makes this description simpler to follow, but we are also going to use it to store those annotations in a query-friendly form. As you can see on that last screenshot, we store the raw JSON data returned by FISE—in the *raw_json* property—as well as our simplified triple notation in the *jcr:title* property of the *obama node* that stores the annotation. Node names like *obama* do not have a specific meaning in this case, they are generated automatically by the Apache Sling (http://sling.apache.org) application layer that we use to interact with JCR, and help make the node hierarchy easy to explore and to understand.

If needed, we could also store the complete JSON-LD data (or another suitable format) returned by FISE, as a property of the node *annotations*. This might be useful in case we do not store all supplied annotations in our micro-tree, to be able to update that micro-tree if we later realize that we ignored too many FISE annotations.

At this point we have a simple and clean structure to store annotations supplied by FISE that can be added to our existing CMS content with no other configuration or content changes. Semantic purists might not like the loss of information that occurs when mapping a well-defined entity type to a simple string like *Person* for storage. But if we can limit ourselves to a relatively small set of entity types, we will be fine, and storing our annotations in this form makes them easy to understand by the *semantic layman*, and as we will see easy to query as well.

4.4.4 Simplified Semantic Queries

The standard JCR query system allows us, among other things, to query for string and substring values in JCR properties. Simple Boolean expressions are supported; see the JCR specification, which is surprisingly readable, for more information. To keep things simple we will just express our example queries in a simplified form here, but the real JCR queries would not be much more complicated.

4.4.5 Searching for Semantic Annotations

A simple search for the *Person:Barack Obama* string would find annotation nodes that refer to that entity. The query would also return nodes that contain the text *Person:Barack Obama* in another context, for example, the text of this chapter if it was stored in our content repository.

To select only annotation nodes, we can add a JCR mixin to them, and add the necessary JCR query statements to our queries to return only nodes that have this mixin. A mixin is a partial JCR node type definition that can be added to a node in addition to its primary JCR node type definition. In our case, the mixin will not define any constraints on the node. It is just a marker that indicates that the node is a semantic annotation, which makes it easy and efficient to restrict our result set when querying for annotations. We could also use a JCR node type instead of a mixin to identify annotations, but at this early stage of our design a mixin is more flexible, especially if it does not impose any constraints on annotation nodes.

4.4.6 Searching for Pages that Reference a Given Entity or Set of Entities

Having added a mixin query restriction as described in the section above, a corresponding query for *Person:Barack Obama* would find all CMS pages that refer to Mr. Obama. If we generate our simplified annotation strings in a predictable way from the RDF triples provided by FISE (see below), we can guarantee that all such entities will use this notation for their annotations.

The net result is that within our restricted simplified ontology this query precisely points to a well-defined set of entities returned by FISE, without requiring any additional tools than what JCR provides out of the box.

4.4.7 Searching for Related Pages

To search for related pages, we just need to build a query from all the semantic annotations of the source page, and OR those search terms.

Searching for *Person:Barack Obama OR Organization:United Nations OR Location:Geneva*, for example, with the mixin restriction mentioned above, will return pages where FISE provides at least one of these annotations. JCR query results are ranked, so pages that have several of those annotations will be at the beginning of the result set. This requires aggregating all the annotation strings of a content item for indexing, which can be done either by configuration at the JCR level, or at the application level.

This should be sufficient to implement a simple semantic-based similarity search, assuming of course that FISE returns meaningful annotations. As in the previous example, this works by using JCR out of the box, with no additional tools.

4.4.8 Is it that Simple?

The two simple query examples shown above can be used as basic semantic building blocks to implement our use cases, and it seems like they are all we need at this point. Even without the full power of SPARQL or other semantic queries, semantic annotations will definitely add value to our content store.

4.4.9 Mapping RDF Triples to our Simplified Notation

We have not yet discussed how the RDF triples returned by FISE get converted to their simplified form (like *Person:Barack Obama*). The component that implements this mapping will need to be aware of the ontologies used by FISE, to supply meaningful conversions and provide reliable mappings. However, if we limit ourselves to a small set of entity types like Person, Organization, Event, Place, Theme and Language, it should be possible to define simple automatic mappings that work in the large majority of cases. To go one step further, the mapper should allow a list of hints to be configured, to help fix suboptimal annotation entity names that might appear in our content repository due to automatic mappings. As we are storing the original RDF triples returned by FISE, the mapper can run again on problematic annotations to fix them later if needed.

4.5 Closing Comments

4.5.1 Risks and Challenges

Assuming FISE works as promised, which is very likely to happen as the IKS/Stanbol community (http://www.iks-project.eu, http://incubator.apache.org/stanbol/) grows and people start using it in production, we will get good quality annotations out of the box. Some tuning of the content enhancement engines might be needed, but we can count on the IKS/Stanbol community to help, assuming everybody will have similar concerns. The Integration of FISE with our CMS should be straightforward, as its OSGi-based architecture is very similar to the one we use in our products including a number of common components. We might run FISE as a separate process, or integrate it as in-process services to simplify deployment. No unknowns here, we will just need to experiment a bit to find the optimal solution. The bulk of our work seems to reside in the mapper that converts RDF triples to our simplified notation. This needs to produce human-readable annotations without losing data, which does not seem too complex but will need serious automated testing to validate the mapping algorithms. The very last step is to test this on a repository with a meaningful amount of content, and define a number of test queries to validate the overall quality and added value. This is not risky or complex, but the testing effort should not be underestimated, as it takes time to come up with a good number of meaningful tests.

4.5.2 Semantic Content Enrichment and Mining in CMS

In the beginning there was static content. Website owners happily edited HTML pages directly, using text editors if needed, and all was good. Websites only contained small numbers of pages, and managing them as a collection of files was perfectly good. The CMS industry quickly moved to database-driven websites, however, initially for websites that contained semi-structured data such as product descriptions, and later for all websites, as a way of separating content from presentation.

The next step was user-generated content, also known as Web 2.0. Moving from a one-directional information broadcast to conversations between website owners and their users, and directly between users, has led to the creation of the conversational Web that we have today. All this additional content requires sophisticated management tools that were initially using relational databases. Today they use increasingly more specialized content repositories like JCR that offer a lot of content-related functionality out of the box.

Now, as seen in the use cases that we describe in this chapter, enhancing content with semantic metadata that is not created directly by content but generated or suggested by somewhat intelligent semantic engines is the next step. Content mining comes alongside with this, as a way of making sense of and correlating diverse content sources, including real-time streams from Twitter or Facebook.

4.6 Conclusion

The tools and techniques described in this chapter provide simple ways of enhancing JCR-based or other content repositories, using sophisticated semantic tools hidden behind simple RESTful interfaces. By voluntarily limiting our semantic functionality to a subset that CMS developers can immediately use, without having to learn new skills or tools, we will provide simple yet value-adding semantic enhancements that leverage the FISE annotation engine and other tools that the IKS team is working on. While going *fully semantic* has its uses for new types of content management applications and for developers who have the required skills, we believe that bridging techniques like the one we presented here will help advance the state of the art in an evolutionary way: not revolutionary but immediately useful, understandable and with minimal added complexity.

References

1. Delacretaz, B.: Semantic image similarities with FISE (2010). URL http://dev.day.com/content/ddc/blog/2010/06/semantic_image_simil.html

2. FISE: Furtwangen iks semantic engine (2010). URL http://wiki.iks-project.eu/index.php/FISE
3. Jackrabbit Wiki: David's model: A guide for content modelling (2010). URL http://wiki.apache.org/jackrabbit/DavidsModel

Biographical Notes

Bertrand Delacretaz works as a senior developer in Day Software's R&D group (http://www.day.com, now part of Adobe), using open source tools to create world-class content management systems. Bertrand is a member and director of the Apache software foundation, and has been or is involved in a number of Apache projects as a committer, project management committee member and incubation mentor.

Dr. Michael Marth works for Day Software (now part of Adobe) as Technology Evangelist promoting content technologies like JCR and Apache Sling. He has been in the content management systems industry for 10 years and held various positions at vendors and integrators. His current interests include content management user interfaces, content mining and natural language processing.

Chapter 5
Dynamic Semantic Publishing

Jem Rayfield

Abstract This chapter describes the transformational technology strategy the BBC Future Media & Technology department is using to evolve from a relational content model and static publishing framework to a fully dynamic semantic publishing (DSP) architecture. This approach uses linked data technology to automate the aggregation, publishing and re-purposing of interrelated content objects according to an ontological domain-modelled information architecture. Providing a greatly improved user experience and high levels of user engagement. The DSP architecture curates and publishes HTML and RDF [1] aggregations based on embedded Linked Data identifiers, ontologies and associated inference. RDF semantics improve navigation, content re-use, re-purposing, search engine rankings, journalist determined levels of automation (*edited by exception*) and support semantic advertisement placement for audiences outside of the UK. The DSP approach facilitates multi-dimensional entry points and a richer navigation, greatly improving user experience and levels of engagement.

Jem Rayfield
Senior Technical Architect, British Broadcasting Corporation (BBC), United Kingdom, e-mail: jem.rayfield@bbc.co.uk

[1] Resource Description Framework (RDF) is based upon the idea of making statements about concepts/resources in the form of subject-predicate-object expressions. These expressions are known as triples in RDF terminology. The subject denotes the resource; and the predicate denotes traits or aspects of the resource and expresses a relationship between the subject and the object. For example, to represent the notion *Frank Lampard plays for England* in RDF is as a triple, the subject is *Frank Lampard*; the predicate is *plays for* and the object is *England Squad*. Further details: Resource Description Framework (RDF) – W3C standard. Retrieved December 4, 2010, from http://www.w3.org/RDF/

5.1 Introduction

BBC News, BBC Sport [2] and over one hundred other web sites across the BBC are authored and published using an in-house bespoke content management/production system (CPS) with an associated static publishing delivery chain. Journalists are able to author stories, manage indices and edit audio/video assets in the CPS and then publish them pre-baked as static assets to the BBC's Apache web server farm. In addition, Journalists can edit and manage content in the CPS for distribution to the BBC Mobile [3] and Interactive TV services, and even for Ceefax[4]. The CPS has been constantly evolving since it was developed to publish the BBC News website, which launched in November 1997, and the latest version (Version 6) underpins the summer 2010 redesign of the BBC News site that won the .net *Redesign of the Year*.

The first significant move away from the CPS static publishing model by the BBC's Future Media & Technology (FM&T) department was through the creation of the BBC Sport World Cup 2010 website[5]. From first using the site, the most striking changes are the horizontal navigation and the larger format high-quality video. As you navigate through the site it becomes apparent that this is a far deeper and richer use of content than can be achieved through a traditional CMS and associate relational model and static publishing solution.

The BBC World Cup 2010 site features 700-plus team, group and player pages, which are powered by a high-performance dynamic semantic publishing (DSP) architecture. Previously, BBC Sport would never have considered creating this number of indices in the CPS, as each index would need an editor to keep it up to date with the latest stories, even where automation rules had been set up. To put this scale of task into perspective, the World Cup site has more index pages than the rest of the BBC Sport site.

The DSP architecture enabled the publication of automated metadata[6]-driven web pages that require minimal journalist management, as they automatically aggregate and render links to relevant stories and assets. The underlying aggregation-publishing framework does not author content directly; rather it publishes data about the content—metadata. The published metadata describes the World Cup 2010 content at a fairly low-level of granularity, providing rich content relationships and semantic navigation; querying the published metadata enables the creation of dynamic page aggregations.

---

[2] http://www.bbc.co.uk/news/ and http://news.bbc.co.uk/sport/

[3] http://www.bbc.co.uk/mobile/

[4] BBC's teletext service transmitted by an analogue television signal http://en.wikipedia.org/wiki/Ceefax

[5] The BBC World Cup 2010 web site powered by the DSP architecture http://news.bbc.co.uk/sport1/hi/football/world_cup_2010/default.stm

[6] Metadata is data about data—it describes other data. In this instance, it provides information about the content of a digital asset. For example, a World Cup story may include metadata that describes which football players are mentioned within the text of a story. The metadata may also describe the associated team, group or organization associated to the story.

5 Dynamic Semantic Publishing 51

The World Cup 2010 website created multi-dimensional entry points for Players, Teams, Groups, Matches and provided a much improved and more engaging way for users to explore BBC content when compared to the previous model of flat archive pages.

In the next year or so, a number of BBC sites will be published using the DSP model, including a redesigned and refreshed BBC Sport site, the London 2012 Olympics site and local BBC News sites based around geographical aggregation. All content objects and aggregations will be served and rendered on a dynamic request-by-request basis—as opposed to simple metadata aggregation—to support rich navigation, state changes such as event or time and, potentially, personalisation; with the information architecture and page layout reacting to underlying semantics and state change.

The process by which the BBC intends to evolve the static publishing CPS and the semantic annotation and dynamic metadata publication used for BBC World Cup web site towards its eventual goal of a fully dynamic semantic publishing architecture is described in the following sections.

5.2 Static Publishing and CPS CMS

The CPS has been designed and developed in-house, and so its workflow and process model has evolved to its current form (Version 6) through continuous iteration and feedback from the BBC Journalists who use it to author and publish content for the BBC News and Sport websites. When looking at the requirements for the recently redesigned and refreshed News site, the FM&T department considered evaluating proprietary and open-source solutions in the CMS market for shiny new features. However an interesting thing about the CPS is that most BBC journalists who use it value it very highly. Compared to my experience with many organisations and their CMS it does a pretty decent job.

The CPS client is built using Microsoft .Net 3.5 and takes full advantage of the Windows Presentation Foundation (WPF)[7] toolset. The screen shots of the CPS User Interface (UI) as depicted in Fig. 5.1 illustrate some its features such as the story-editing and index-editing window.

The CPS has a number of tools supporting its story-editing functions such as managing site navigation, associating stories to indices and others such as search. As you can see there is a component-based structure to the story content with a video, introduction and a quote shown. These components are pre-defined allowing a journalist to drag and drop as desired. It is clear that the UI is not a WYSIWIG[8] editor. The current incarnation of the CPS focuses on content structure rather than presentation or content metadata. Although the editor is not WYSIWIG CPS content is available for preview and indeed publication to a number of audience facing out-

---

[7] http://en.wikipedia.org/wiki/Windows_Presentation_Foundation
[8] What You See Is What You Get: http://en.wikipedia.org/wiki/WYSIWYG

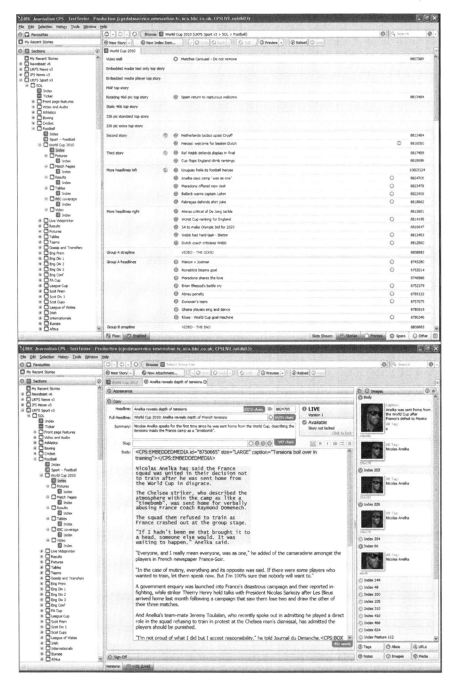

Fig. 5.1: BBC CPS CMS Story editor (top) and Index editor (bottom)

5 Dynamic Semantic Publishing   53

puts and associated devices. On publication CPS assets are statically rendered for audience-facing output—flavours include RSS, Atom, High-Web XHTML, Low-Web XHTML and mobile outputs.

The static CPS delivery architecture, as depicted in Fig. 5.2, provides a highly scalable and high performance static content object-publishing framework. The CPS UI utilises a Microsoft .Net Windows Communication Foundation (WCF)[9] data layer Application Programming Interface (API) abstraction which proxies the underlying persistence mechanism (relational database management system from Oracle). The abstracted relational data model captures and persists stories and media assets as well as site structure and associated page layout. The CPS UI allows the journalist to author stories, media and site structure for preview, eventual publication and re-publication. A daemon process, the CPS publisher, subscribes to publication events for processing and delivery. The CPS publisher contextualises content objects in order that they are appropriate for required audience / platform output. Filtered, contextualised assets are rendered by the CPS publisher MVC[10] as a static file per output type. Each output representation is made persistent onto a Storage Area Network (SAN). The BBC's home grown content delivery chain subscribes to SAN changes and publishes each output from a secure content creation network onto a set of head Apache HTTPd (http://httpd.apache.org/) servers accessible to the audience.

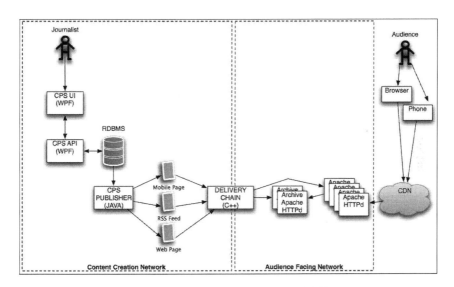

Fig. 5.2: BBC News – CPS static publishing

---

[9] http://en.wikipedia.org/wiki/Windows_Communication_Foundation

[10] Model View Controller (MVC) is an architectural pattern that isolates domain logic from presentation logic

Although the CPS relational content model and static publishing mechanism scales and performs well it has a number of functional limitations. CPS authored content has a fixed association to manually administered indices and outputs are fixed in time without any consideration to asset semantics, state changes or semantic metadata. Re-using and re-purposing CPS authored content to react to different scenarios is very difficult due to the static nature of its output representations. Re-purposing content within a semantic context driven by metadata is impossible without manual Journalist management and re-publishing. Manual complex data management inevitably leads to time, expense and data administration headaches.

The CPS relational data model currently has a very simple metadata model capturing basic items such as author, publish date and site section. Extending the CPS relational content model to support a rich metadata model becomes complex. When designing a knowledge domain annotation schema using a relational approach one can start by trying to create a flat controlled vocabulary, which can be associated to content objects. However, this quickly breaks, as semantics are very unclear. Evolving this further, a flat controlled vocabulary can be grouped into vocabulary categories; nevertheless, a restrictive and hierarchal taxonomical annotation schema soon evolves again. As concepts need to be shared this gives rise to vocabulary repetition and ambiguity. A taxonomic hierarchy further evolves into a graph, allowing concepts to be shared and re-used to ensure that semantics are disambiguous and knowledge is concise.

Implementing a categorised controlled vocabulary within a relational database introduces complexity; creating a hierarchy introduces further complexity, and implementing graph theory within a relation model takes things past the useable limits of a relational model. If you then add in requirements for reasoning based on metadata semantics then relational databases, associated SQL and schemas are no longer applicable solutions and are simply redundant in this problem space.

5.3 Dynamic Semantic Annotation Driven Publishing

The primary goals of the World Cup 2010 web site were to promote the quality of the original, authored in-house BBC content in context and to increase its visibility and longevity by improving the breadth and depth of navigational functionality. Increasing user journeys through the range of content while keeping the audience engaged on the site meant that a larger more complex information architecture was required than that traditionally managed by BBC Journalists. Creating a website navigation for 700+ Players, Teams, Groups and Matches pages posed a problem as the traditional CPS manual content administration processes would not scale. An automated solution was required in order that a small number of Journalists could author and surface the content with as light a touch as possible; and automatically aggregate content onto the 700+ pages based on the concepts and semantics contained within the body of the story documents.

5 Dynamic Semantic Publishing

The information architecture gave rise to a domain model which included concepts and relationships such as time and location; events and competitions; groups, leagues and divisions; stages and rounds; matches; teams, squads and players; players within squads, teams playing in groups, groups within stages, etc.

Clearly, the sport domain soon gives rise to a fairly complex metadata model. When you then include a model that describes the assets that need to be aggregated with a semantic association to the sport domain, it is quickly apparent that using a relational database is not an appropriate solution. The BBC needed to evolve beyond a relational CPS static architecture.

As described above, the DSP architecture and its underlying publishing framework publish metadata. For the World Cup, the published metadata described the content at a fairly low-level of granularity, providing rich content relationships and semantic navigation. By querying this published metadata we were able to create automatic dynamic page aggregations for Teams, Groups and Players.

The foundation of these dynamic aggregations was a rich ontological domain model. The ontology described entity existence, groups and relationships between the things/concepts that describe the World Cup. For example, *Frank Lampard* was part of the *England Squad* and the *England Squad* competed in *Group C* of the *FIFA World Cup 2010*.

The ontology model also described journalist-authored assets—stories, blogs, profiles, images, video and statistics—and enabled them to be associated to concepts within the domain model. Thus a story with an *England Squad* concept relationship provides the basis for a dynamic query aggregation for the England Squad page *All stories tagged with England Squad* (cf. Fig. 5.3[11]).

The required domain ontology was broken down into three basic areas: asset, tag and domain ontologies (cf. Fig. 5.4). They form a triple and thus, allow a Journalist to apply a triple-set to a static asset, such as associating the concept *Frank Lampard* with a story *Goal re-ignites technology row*. The tagging ontology was kept deliberately simple in order to protect the Journalist from the complexities of the underlying domain model. A simple set of asset / domain joining predicates, such as *about* and *mentions*, drive the annotation tool UI and workflow, keeping the annotation simple and efficient, without losing any of the power of the associated knowledge model.

In addition to a manual selective tagging process, Journalist-authored content is automatically analysed against the domain ontology. A natural language determiner process automatically extracts concepts embedded within a textual representation of a story. The concepts are moderated and, again, selectively applied before publication. Moderated, automated concept analysis improves the depth, breadth and quality of metadata publishing.

The screen shots depicted in Fig. 5.5 describe the process of content annotation. The first, applying a story with a sport concept, in this case the story is about the football player *Gareth Barry* (Fig. 5.5, top). In the second instance, the Journalist annotates a story with the location *Milton Keynes* (Fig. 5.5, bottom), where a serious

---

[11] http://news.bbc.co.uk/sport1/hi/football/world_cup_2010/groups_and_teams/team/england

Fig. 5.3: Dynamic RDF automated England index

newsworthy accident has occurred. The journalist applies suggested annotations as well as searching for triple store indexed concepts. As you can see all ontology concepts are linked to linked-open data (LOD)[12] identifiers (DBPedia, GeoNames etc.), allowing a Journalist to correctly disambiguate concepts such as football players or geographical locations.

Journalist-published metadata is captured and made persistent for querying using the RDF metadata representation and triple store (BigOWLIM[13]) technology. Figure 5.6 depicts the dynamic semantic architecture built to publish metadata driven static asset aggregations. RDF triple store[14] and SPARQL[15] approaches were chosen over and above traditional relational database technologies due to the requirements for interpretation of metadata with respect to an ontological domain model. The high-level goal is that the domain ontology allows for intelligent mapping of

---

[12] The term Linked Open Data (LOD) is used to describe a method of exposing, sharing, and connecting data via dereference-able URIs on the Web.

[13] A high performance, scalable, resilient triple store with robust OWL reasoning support

[14] A database for the storage and retrieval of RDF metadata

[15] Pronounced "sparkle"; It is a recursive acronym that stands for SPARQL Protocol and RDF Query Language

5 Dynamic Semantic Publishing

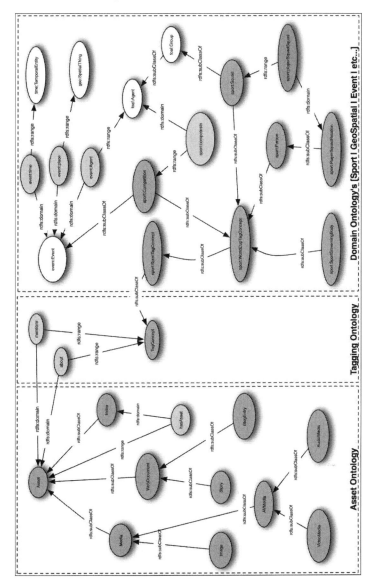

Fig. 5.4: The Asset, Tag and Domain Ontologies used in the World Cup 2010. Note: The full details of the depicted ontologies are not included for brevity.

journalist assets to concepts and queries. The chosen triple-store provides reasoning following the forward-chaining model and thus implicitly inferred statements are automatically derived from the explicitly applied journalist metadata concepts. For example, if a journalist selects and applies the single concept Frank Lampard, then the framework infers and applies concepts such as *England Squad, Group C and*

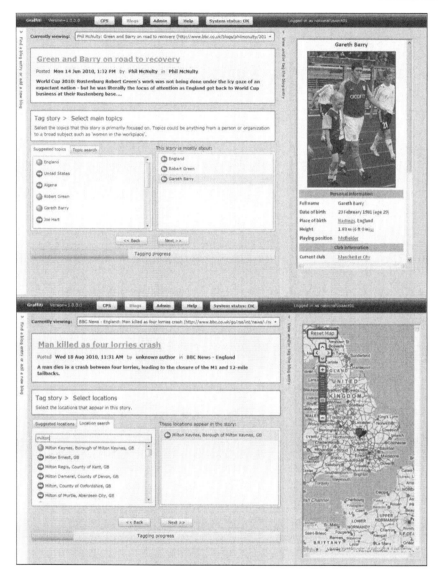

Fig. 5.5: Graffiti annotation tool UI

FIFA World Cup 2010 (as generated triples within the triple store). Thus the semantics of the ontologies, the factual data, and the content metadata are taken into account during query evaluation. The triple-store was configured so that it performed reasoning with the semantics of all this data—at real time, hundreds of updates per minute while millions of concurrent requests occur against the same database.

5 Dynamic Semantic Publishing

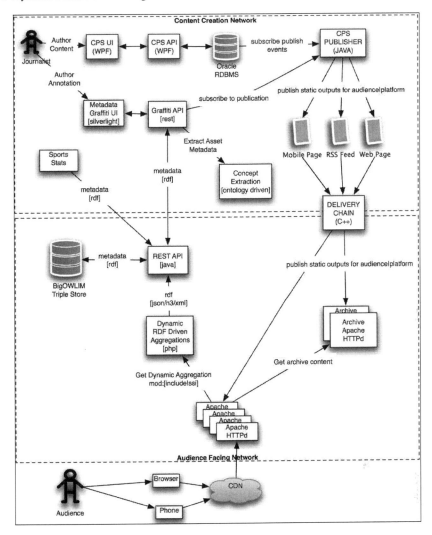

Fig. 5.6: Semantic World Cup 2010 publishing powered by a triple store

This inference capability makes both the journalist tagging and the triple store powered SPARQL queries simpler and indeed quicker than a traditional SQL approach. Dynamic aggregations based on inferred statements increase the quality and breadth of content across the site. The RDF triple approach also facilitates agile modelling, whereas traditional relational schema modelling is less flexible and also increases query complexity.

The BBC triple store is deployed multi-data centre in a resilient, clustered, high-performance and horizontally scalable fashion, allowing future expansion for additional domain ontologies and if required, LOD sets.

The triple store is abstracted via a Java, Spring (http://www.springsource.org/), Apache CXF (http://cxf.apache.org/) or JSR311 (http://jsr311.java.net/) compliant REST service. The REST API is accessible via HTTPs with an appropriate certificate. The API is designed as a generic façade onto the triple-store allowing RDF data to be re-purposed and re-used pan BBC. This service orchestrates SPARQL queries and ensures that results are dynamically cached with a low, one minute 'time-to-live' (TTL) expiry cross data centre using memcached[16].

All RDF metadata transactions sent to the API for CRUD operations are validated against associated ontologies before any persistence operations are invoked. This validation process ensures that RDF conforms to underlying ontologies and ensures data consistency. The validation libraries used include Jena Eyeball[17]. The API also performs content transformations between the various flavours of RDF such as N3 or XML RDF.

Automated XML sports stats feeds from various sources are delivered and processed by the BBC. These feeds are now also transformed into an RDF representation. The transformation process maps feed-supplier IDs onto corresponding ontology concepts and thus aligns external provider data with the RDF ontology representation with the triple store. Sports stats for Matches, Teams and Players are aggregated inline and served dynamically from the persistent triple store.

The dynamic aggregation and publishing page-rendering layer is built using a Zend PHP[18] and memcached stack. The PHP layer requests an RDF representation of a particular concept or concepts from the REST service layer based on the audience's URL request. If an *England Squad* page request is received by the PHP code several RDF queries will be invoked over HTTPs to the REST service layer below.

To make use of the architecture significant number of existing static news kit and architecture (Apache servers, HTTP load balancers and gateway architecture) all HTTP responses are annotated with appropriate low (one minute) cache expires headers. This HTTP caching increases the scalability of the platform and also allows Content Delivery Network (CDN)[19] caching if demand requires.

The DSP architecture served millions of page requests a day throughout the World Cup with continually changing OWL[20] reasoned semantic RDF data. It served an average of a million SPARQL queries per day for the duration of tournament, with a peak RDF transaction rate of 100s of Player statistics per minute. Cache expiry at all layers within the framework is one minute enabling a dynamic, rapidly changing domain and statistic-driven user experience.

---

[16] Distributed memory caching system

[17] Java RDF validation library for checking ontological issues with RDF: http://jena.sourceforge.net/Eyeball/

[18] Open source scripting virtual machine for PHP: http://www.zend.com

[19] Content Delivery Network or Content Distribution Network (CDN) is a collection of computers usually hosted within Internet Service Provider hosting facilities. The CDN servers cache local copies of content to maximize bandwidth and reduce requests to origin servers.

[20] Web Ontology Language (OWL): http://www.w3.org/2004/OWL/

5.4 Fully Dynamic Publishing

Although the World Cup 2010 architecture enables static asset content aggregation and re-purposing based on dynamic triple-store RDF metadata it does not support dynamic asset rendering. Assets such as stories are fixed and immutable. Upcoming BBC projects such, as the Olympics 2012 require content objects to be cut-up, arranged and rendered with respect to state changes and persona. The ability to render content object fragments by state and indeed metadata concept will enable the Olympics 2012 web site to facilitate personalised, event driven pages for Olympic athletes, stadiums, events and teams with greater flexibility than that achieved for the World Cup 2010 web site.

The DSP architecture as shown in Fig. 5.7 now takes a final evolution deprecating the static, fixed asset publication in preference for dynamic content object renditions. Content objects are dynamically rendered on a request-by-request basis rather than fixed-in-time static publication. Textual content objects are made persistent within a schema independent content store, supporting fine-grained XQuery[21], search, versioning and access control. The content store is horizontally scalable and allows content to be handled in discreet chunks supporting fine-grained content cut up and re-purposing. Each content object within the content store is modelled as a discrete document with no interrelationships.

Discrete content objects are to be modelled and referenced via the asset ontologyRDF within the triple-store. Triple-store SPARQL is used to locate, query and search for documents by concept providing all the aggregation and inference functionality required. The content store is used for fast, scalable query-able and searchable access to the raw content object data while the triple-store continues to provide access to asset references and associated domain models.

The Graffiti annotation tool UI makes it possible for a journalist to annotate static content objects post-publication. However, it does not integrate with the CPS UI. Using the Graffiti API within the CPS UI unifies and rationalises the Journalists' toolset. Merging the Graffiti UI into the CPS UI provides a single UI for the Journalist, supporting the creation and annotation of documents within a single view. Real-time concept extraction and suggestion occurs as the Journalist authors and then publishes content.

Sports statistics provided by third party agencies are now to be stored as XML content within the query-able content store. The triple store will be used in a purer sense and will only be concerned with domain and asset metadata—it will not persist or manage content object data. Third party statistic identifiers are to be mapped to sport ontology concepts thus allowing querying across the triple-store and content store for sports statistics related to a sport concept, e.g., *The league table for the English Premiership*. This allows content objects and sports statistics to be cut up and arranged on a personalised, metadata driven, request-by-request basis.

The triple-store and content store are to be abstracted and orchestrated by a REST API. The API will continue to support SPARQL and RDF validation how-

---

[21] A query and functional programming language: http://www.w3.org/XML/Query/

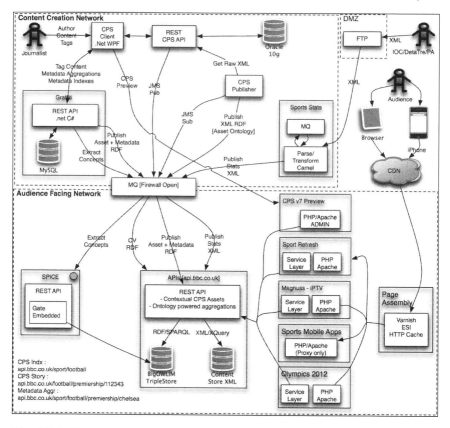

Fig. 5.7: DSP architecture combining SPARQL/XQuery. Note: ZXTM HTTP LBs are not included for clarity

ever it will now support a transactional manager across both the triple-store and the content store. Allowing a content aggregation to be generated using a combination of SPARQL for domain querying and XQuery for asset selection. All content object and metadata will be made persistent in transactional manner across both data sources.

Figure 5.8 depicts the content API TRiPOD that makes use of a multi-data centre memcached cluster to store content aggregations and protect the triple store and content-store from query storms. The API cache is split into a live cache with a low one-minute TTL and a second, longer stale cache with an expiry TTL of 48 hours. Memcache is also used to control SPARQL / XQuery invocation using a memcache-based locking strategy. If the live cache has expired a lock is created and a single query invocation thread per data centre is invoked. Subsequent requests are served from stale until the query responds refreshing both the stale and live cache.

The DSP platform caching approach is fundamental to enable a scalable and high-performance platform. The API memcache strategy is augmented with HTTP

5 Dynamic Semantic Publishing

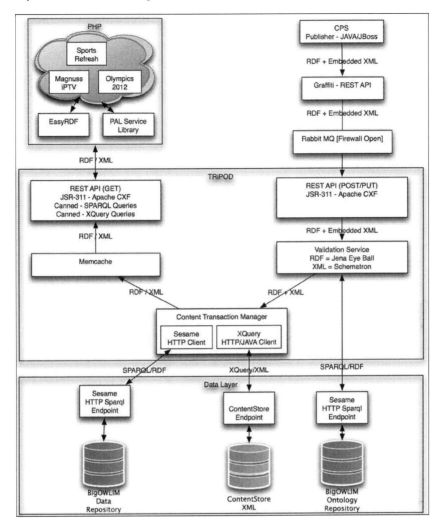

Fig. 5.8: DSP software stack

caching between the PHP render layer and the API. The PHP layer also makes use of memcache for page module caching; all page fragments are cached at a Varnish ESI[22] page assembly layer with corresponding HTTP caching. The site as a whole is also edge-cached for further scalability and resilience during very large traffic spikes.

---

[22] Edge Side Include (ESI) markup language used in headend/edge web servers dynamic web content assembly. ESI supports caching and aims to tackle web infrastructure scaling.

5.5 Conclusion

A technical architecture that combines a document / content store with a triple-store proves an excellent data and metadata persistence layer for any CMS. A triple-store provides a concise, accurate and clean implementation methodology for describing domain knowledge models. An RDF graph approach provides ultimate modelling expressivity, with the added advantage of deductive reasoning. SPARQL simplifies domain queries, with the associated underlying RDF schema being more flexible than a corresponding SQL / RDBMS approach. A document / content store provides schema flexibility; schema independent storage; versioning, and search and query facilities across atomic content objects. Combining a model expressed as RDF referencing content objects in a scalable document / content-store provides a persistence layer that uses the best of both technical approaches. This combination removes the shackles associated with traditional RDBMS approaches. Using each data store for what it is best at creates a framework that scales and is ultimately flexible.

Replacing a static publishing mechanism with a dynamic request-by-request solution that uses a scalable metadata / data layer will remove the barriers to creativity for BBC Journalists, Designers and Product Managers, allowing them to make the very best use of the BBC's content. Simplifying the authoring approach via metadata annotation opens this content up and increases the reach and value of the BBC's online content. Finally, combining the triple approach with dynamic atomic documents as an architectural foundation simplifies the publication of pan-BBC content as *open linked data* between BBC systems and across the wider linked open data (LOD) cloud.

Biographical Notes

Jem Rayfield is a Senior Technical architect in the Future Media and Technology division of the British Broadcasting Corporation (BBC), specifically focusing on News, Sport & Knowledge products. This places him at the centre of BBC online architectural strategy and implementation decisions. Prior to working at the BBC, Jem was Technology Director at Razorfish, architecting solutions for numerous clients including O2 and the Financial Times. In his free time, Jem enjoys listening and playing (badly) a wide and eclectic range of music. He also enjoys spending time at the gym.

Chapter 6
Semantics in the Domain of eGovernment

Luis Álvarez Sabucedo and Luis Anido Rifón

Abstract Semantics is becoming a tool of the utmost importance to boost interoperability and accessibility of information in many domains of eTechnologies. eGovernment is not an exception in this unstoppable trend. Actually, for the transition from a paper-based administration to an efficient, paper-less government, a pending challenge for eGovernment activities, an accurate use of semantic tools is required. For example, the semantic annotation of documents provides value-added services to retrieve information and inference processes can be carried out. Key aspects for efficient eGovernment solutions in the future are the provision of a holistic business model, a task tackled in several projects but not yet fully solved as shown in this chapter, and the application of more convenient semantic tools in each public administration process. In this line, lightweight semantics are currently adopted, which are also recommended and discussed in the current chapter with regard to their application to the domain of eGovernment.

6.1 Introduction

Electronic Government (eGovernment) solutions should not simply replace paper-based services with digitally delivered services. On the contrary, when providing solutions to the public sector, it should be carried out a complete and deep reorganization of the governmental processes under investigation. This is rather a revolution in the domain and goes hand-in-hand with new features and possibilities that provide value-added services for citizens, the final users of the newly developed eGovernment solutions. And these solutions can take advantage of semantic web

---

Luis Álvarez Sabucedo
Associate Professor, Universidade de Vigo, Vigo (Pontevedra), Spain, e-mail: Luis.Sabucedo@det.uvigo.es

Luis Anido Rifón,
Full Professor, Universidade de Vigo, Vigo (Pontevedra), Spain, e-mail: lanido@det.uvigo.es

technologies. For example, the adoption of semantic annotations brings outstanding features regarding information retrieval, knowledge discovery and document management. From an appropriate usage of the different possible levels of complexity made available by semantic technologies, e.g. from simple folksonomies and taxonomies (cf. [9]) to complex ontologies (cf. [11]), it is possible to derive innovative options in the fulfillment of public services.

In order to show how that is possible, we will first present a review of the actual concept of eGovernment. We then review state-of-the-art regarding semantics in the domain of eGovernment. Afterwards, we present a model for the integration of semantics into the domain of eGovernment. And finally, conclusions and comments with regard to future projects in this area are given.

6.2 The Domain

During the last couple of years, eGovernment is experiencing a huge development boosted by both demands of citizens for better services and growing requirements imposed by Public Administrations (PAs) to themselves by laws. Developers and stakeholders should not consider an eGovernment solution as a simple replacement of a paper-based administration with electronically driven services. On the contrary, eGovernment solutions should involve a deep transformation of services provided by PAs to citizens. Hereby, it should be considered the change from process-based applications into new paradigms of services that focus on current needs of citizens. This aspect of the problem is clear from the definition, whereby eGovernment refers "to the use by government agencies of information technologies (such as Wide Area Networks, the Internet, and mobile computing) that have the ability to transform relations with citizens, businesses, and other arms" [18].

In order to accomplish this ambitious goal, a deep re-engineering process should be undertaken. In this long-term process one should consider the following three concepts:

- **Interoperability**: Addressed by all major institutions, interoperability must be considered at all phases of the project. Final solutions derived from current initiatives must properly address this feature at different levels, namely, on the technical level, the application level and finally, the semantics level.
- **Accessibility**: The fight against the digital gap is clearly present in the domain of eGovernment. PAs cannot afford to prevent users from using their own solutions for problems related to accessibility or availability.
- **Maintainability**: Solutions in PAs are expected to have a long life cycle. Applications will be in use for a long time. So, maintenance must be taken into account during the design phase and deployment phase of eGovernment solutions.

6.3 Existing Approaches to eGovernment

The eGovernment domain is becoming an area for research where an ever-increasing number of solutions are being proposed and developed. Currently, these solutions include a theoretical characterization of concrete situations. They are aimed at providing a real solution, exploring possibilities and features in the context of a certain framework. In order to have a clear idea of the current state-of-the-art, we can categorize the efforts in the domain into three groups:

1. **Initiatives from governmental bodies**: Since the discussion of first eGovernment solutions, national governments and supra-national organisations such as the European Union have been concerned with interoperability issues. Therefore, they have supported the provision of recommendations and interoperability solutions in the domain.
2. **Standardization bodies and consortia**: International standardization bodies have paid attention to this domain over the last years. Most of their work is related to the adoption of their previous specifications and standards to cover needs that apply to the domain of eGovernment.
3. **Projects developed by research institutions**: Resources assigned to this area by many institutions (e.g. the European Commission), have resulted in a large amount of projects related to eGovernment solutions.

In the following, each approach to eGovernment is described briefly and corresponding examples are provided.

6.3.1 Governmental Initiatives

The vast majority of countries have developed their own frameworks to host eGovernment solutions [10]. Most of them provide frameworks that address interoperability at some level or support tasks related to eGovernment solutions. However, none of them provide a solid or holistic platform to actually carry out eGovernment services. We briefly outline some of those projects:

- **SAGA (Standards und Architekturen in eGovernment Anwendungen) [8] in Germany**: It is a guideline for the development of eGovernment solutions in German PAs. This framework does not take care of semantic-based solutions. It provides a set of standards that must be used to deploy eGovernment solutions.
- **e-GIF (eGovernment Interoperability Framework) in the United Kingdom [17]**: It covers issues related to specifications and policies for any cross-agency collaboration, eService access and content management. It also includes definitions of metadata to mark documents by using RDF [21]. It is one of the official projects that makes larger use of semantic technologies. However, it only uses lightweight semantic technologies.

- **EIF (European Interoperability Framework) for European solutions [6]**: Primarily, it establishes a framework for discussions about interoperability, but it does not actually endorse any particular catalogue or standard to build eGovernment solutions. Anyhow, it supports European countries in finding an interoperable framework for pan-European eGovernment solutions.
- **FEAF (Federal Enterprise Architecture Framework) in USA (CIOC, 1999)**: It focuses on the description of enterprise models to develop cross-border solutions. It does neither take care of particular architectures or technologies, nor does it actually deploy systems. It is quite useful as systematic way to design solutions whereby the business needs of all stakeholders are considered.

Most of these projects provide little semantic support as they just make use of very lightweight semantic technologies at the best. And as the adoption and use of so-called heavy-weight ontologies is an activity to be done at this level, one cannot take full advantage of any approach listed above for future projects. Unfortunately, it must be stated that the support provided by these initiatives to develop actual platforms is limited. Guijarro [10] discusses further details on this topic.

6.3.2 Standardization Bodies

Several international organisations involved in standardization processes have also devoted efforts to eGovernment solutions. Some of the most relevant organisations involved in horizontal technological development have also launched their own particular groups of interest. The most outstanding bodies are listed in the following:

- **DGRC**: The Digital Government Research Center was founded in 1999 by the National Science Foundation [12]. Its area of interest is the investigation of information and communication technologies applied to eGovernment solutions. Several projects have been conducted and the information intended for citizens is provided by means of the newsletter dgOnline [7].
- **OMG**: The Object Management Group [14], together with all the projects and initiatives carried out, launched a specific working group for eGovernment. This group is called Government Domain Task Force (GovDTF). Their primary focus of interest is related to the application of the Model Driven Architecture and other OMG specifications to eGovernment solutions.
- **OASIS**: The Organisation for the Advancement of Structured Information Standards [13] also has a committee that investigates the applicability of their own technologies to the domain of eGovernment. In the first instance, OASIS focuses on the articulation and coordination of requirements for XML-based and Web services-based standards. This Committee includes several subcommittees (SC): eGov Asia-Pacific SC, eGov Best Practices SC, eGov Core Components SC, eGov ebXML Registry SC, eGov Harmonising Taxonomies, eGov Infrastructure SC, eGov Services SC, and eGov Web Services SC.

- **CEN**: The European Committee for Standardization [2] launched its own group of interest in the eGovernment domain in February 2005 [3]. In addition, the group has undertaken some interesting work by means of some CEN Workshop Agreements (CWAs): CWA 1859 "Guidance on the Use of Metadata in E-Government" [5] and CWA 13988 "Guidance information for the use of Dublin Core in Europe" [4].
- **W3C**: The eGovernment Interest Group [19] is a research group hosted by the W3C. It is concerned with improving the access to governmental information through usage of Web standards. Several projects are being carried out such as Linked Data (http://linkeddata.org/) or Government Data Management (http://www.w3.org/egov/wiki/ProjectData).

Even though the work of these groups must be taken into account for the investigation of eGovernment solutions, none of these groups can provide us with a solid foundation for the provision of a semantic description of the eGovernment domain. As a common and shared model of the domain could not be provided across different countries, it is not simple to provide solutions that can collaborate and interchange data in a simple and extensible manner. Barely, agreements on technologies have been *de facto* achieved such as the use of Web Services for service invocation or XML for data exchange.

6.3.3 Projects in the Domain

There are a number of projects that apply semantics to eGovernment solutions. Some of them are already completed and others are work-in-progress. However, from all of them lessons learnt can be derived that can guide future work. We would like to outline some of these projects:

- The Finnish website **Suomi.fi** [16] implements a taxonomy that allows a formal classification of Life Events. This classification represents an artefact from the domain of eGovernment that describes high-level services for citizens from one or several PAs. The provided support is just concerned with the interaction with human users. Unfortunately, no mechanism for automatic invocation of services is provided.
- The **SemanticGov project** [11] is part-funded by the European Commission's Sixth Framework Program. It aims at developing a software infrastructure that supports PAs. The project applies the Web Service Modeling Ontology (WSMO, http://www.wsmo.org/) to provide interoperability mechanisms. The definition of pre-conditions and post-conditions turns out to be quite challenging in this project. However, it provides a two-level ontology that allows a detailed modelling of life events.
- The **Access-eGov project** [1] is also part-funded by the European Commission's Sixth Framework Program. It is based on a peer-to-peer (P2P) and service-oriented architecture (SOA) that also takes advantage of semantic technologies

to improve accessibility and connectivity. It focuses more on reorientation to provide support and access to existing services rather than on the provision of strategies for an automatic composition of services or semantic-based search of services.

6.4 Introducing Semantics in eGovernment Solutions

The eGovernment requirements about interoperability are among the highest for all eTechnologies. This fact is clear from the need of interaction among different PAs in response to the needs of the citizens in the current world. It is therefore not only solid technological support required but also social and political commitment in this long-term bet.

The provision of a common business model that fully characterizes possible interactions in the domain of eGovernment is the very first step. This common business model should, for instance, include information about how to discover a service, how to invoke the desired operation and how to check the status of an invoked operation. These features require a deep interaction at semantic, organizational and infrastructural level.

Consequently, this is not an easy task as we can note from the lack of common understanding in current approaches described above. It is not possible to point out a unique model to support services in the domain. Thus, the provision of a heavy-weight ontology seems to be not a step to perform in the short term.

For the near future, this heavy-weight semantic support seems to be the most likely option, regardless of the particular technology chosen. Nevertheless, for the moment being, we rather suggest the use of so-called light-weighted semantic technologies that draw the attention of the eGovernment community today, too. Due to its simplicity of use and compatibility with already existing Web applications, they are currently being used with success in a number of usage scenarios of PAs. We cannot neglect to mention some applications for these technologies with a promising future as discussed in the following sections.

6.4.1 Annotating Documents

One of the burdens of traditional governments is the management of paper-based documents. This must be addressed throughout the transition towards a fully transactional eGovernment support. Hereby, metadata and even tags in documents turn out to be a successful approach to recover, manage and store information. Support for this task is given by the eGif framework through its catalogue of metadata for annotations.

6.4.2 Describing Services

Even though it is not as mature as the use of metadata in documents, services can be annotated as well. Taking the interface of a Web service for its invocation, the provision of a semantic description will clearly increase the possibilities for the accessibility of services.

Consistent with the approach of SA-WSDL [20], the official recommendation from W3C for semantic service descriptions, it requires little effort to include annotations about services and its capabilities. One of the reasons hindering the adoption of SA-WSDL lies not in the immaturity of this technology but in the lack of the above mentioned common business model.

Once this shortcoming has been overcome, the discovery and orchestration of services during runtime will be possible. Then, features with regard to interoperability and collaboration among services will be greatly increased.

6.4.3 Social Services

A pending set of features for eGovernment sites are related to social capabilities, understood in the sense of the Web 2.0 discussion [15]. eGovernment platforms could largely benefit from the inclusion of services related to this trend. Collaborative tagging (e.g., delicious http://www.delicious.com), sharing resources (e.g., Scribd, http://www.scribd.com) and similar features from the Web 2.0 are not yet fully explored for current eGovernment solutions. But the integration of semantic support into those solutions—and even in a simple manner—is highly recommended as it makes search of relevant information more convenient.

Regarding the social interaction aspect of this approach, some initiatives such as the Twitter account of *Gabinete SEC* (Madrid, Spain http://twitter.com/desdelamoncloa) can be mentioned. This account is used by the Spanish Government to inform about the everyday tasks of the government. The use of classic social networks is also a field open to exploration. Nevertheless, it is required to pay attention to some concerns that may arise regarding privacy, personal information protection and others when dealing with social networks applied to this domain, in particular when pre-existing corporative and non-open social networks are used.

6.5 Conclusion

The last years have shown that eGovernment solutions evolved with high speed. Nevertheless, there is still a pending step regarding the use of semantic support for those solutions. Even though projects are undertaken that use semantics for services in eGovernment solutions, there are still many drawbacks. It is currently not possible to point out a broadly accepted business model for services. But this would be the first and most important step towards a semantics-based framework in the eGovernment domain. The development of such a business model will eventually happen, as the domain gets more mature.

In the meantime, eGovernment solutions are rather based on lightweight semantics and annotating services and documents was successful so far. Also, we recognize first eGovernment solutions that use semantic technologies for a search functionality that covers services and documents of PAs. In the near future, social features such as tag clouds or social bookmarking are expected to emerge in eGovernment solutions, too.

References

1. Access-egov project (2010). URL http://www.accessegov.org/
2. European Committee for Standardization (2010). URL http://www.cen.eu/cen/pages/default.aspx
3. European Committee for Standardization: Focus group on e-government (2010). URL http://www.cen.eu/cen/Sectors/Sectors/ISSS/Activity/Pages/e-Government.aspx
4. European Committee for Standardization: Guidance information for the use of dublin core in europe (2010). URL ftp://cenftp1.cenorm.be/PUBLIC/CWAs/e-Europe/MMI-DC/cwa13988-00-2003-Apr.pdf
5. European Committee for Standardization: Guidance on the use of metadata in egovernment (2010). URL http://www.cen.eu/cen/Sectors/Sectors/ISSS/CEN%20Workshop%20Agreements/Pages/CWA14859.aspx
6. European Union: European interoperability framework for pan-european egovernment services (2010). URL http://www.fsfe.org/projects/os/eifv2.en.html
7. Information Science Institute: dgonline (2010). URL http://www.dgrc.org/outreach/dgonline_latest.jsp
8. Kbst: Standards und Architekturen für E-Government (SAGA) (2010). URL http://www.cio.bund.de/DE/Standards/SAGA/saga_node.html
9. Opening up government (2011). URL http://data.gov.uk/linked-data
10. Guijarro, C.L.: Analysis of the interoperability frameworks in e-government initiatives. In: Proceedings of EGOV'04. Saragossa, Spain (2004)
11. Loutas, N., Peristeras, V., Tarabanis, K.: Providing public services to citizens at the national and pan-european level using semantic web technologies: The semanticgov project. In: Procededings of the Sixth Eastern European eGov Days. Czech Republic (2008)
12. National Science Foundation: (2010). URL http://www.nsf.gov/
13. OASIS: (2010). URL http://www.oasis-open.org/
14. OMG: Government DTF (2010). URL http://egov.omg.org/
15. O'Reilly, T.: What is web 2.0 – design patterns and business models for the next generation of software (2005). URL http://oreilly.com/web2/archive/what-is-web-20.html
16. Suomi.fi: One address for citizen's services (2010). URL http://www.suomi.fi/suomifi/english/services_by_topic/index.html
17. UK GovTalk: (2010). URL http://www.cabinetoffice.gov.uk/govtalk/policydocuments/e-gif.aspx
18. World Bank: World bank egovernment (2010). URL http://www.worldbank.org/egov
19. World Wide Web Consortium: egovernment interest group at w3c (2010). URL http://www.w3.org/egov/
20. World Wide Web Consortium: Semantic annotations for wsdl working group (2010). URL http://www.w3.org/2002/ws/sawsdl/
21. World Wide Web Consortium: RDF Vocabulary Description Language 1.0: RDF Schema (2010a). URL http://www.w3.org/TR/rdf-schema/

Biographical Notes

Luis Álvarez Sabucedo has a Telecommunication Engineering degree with honours (2001) and a Telecommunication Engineering PhD with honours (2008) by the Universidade de Vigo. Actually, he is an Associate Professor in the Telematics Engineering Department of the University of Vigo. His research interests include semantic technologies, web-based solutions and eGovernment. His results have been published in several fora such as international conferences and journals. Also, he is involved in a number of national and international research projects.

Luis Anido Rifón has a Telecommunication Engineering degree with honours (1997) in the Telematics and Communication branches and a Telecommunication Engineering PhD with honours (2001) by the Universidade de Vigo. Currently, he is Full Professor in the Telematics Engineering Department of the Universidade de Vigo and holds the post of Director of the Innovation in Education Unit of the University of Vigo. He has received several awards by the W3C, the Royal Academy of Sciences and the Oficial Spanish Telecommunication Association. He has authored more than 180 papers in journals and conferences. He is also technical secretariat of the CTN71 SC36 group of the Spanish Association for Standardisation and Certification (AENOR) and head of the Spanish delegation to ISO/IEC JTC1 SC36.

Chapter 7
The Interactive Knowledge Stack (IKS): A Vision for the Future of CMS

Wernher Behrendt

Abstract We position IKS by looking at where Content Management Systems (CMSs) come from, historically and we discuss where they are at present in the light of large-scale social media applications. We argue that the most prominent issue *semantic search* may be misleading when discussing the future of CMS and we then explore the technical and business-related tensions between CMS, social media, database technology and knowledge-based systems. We then present the conceptual framework of IKS with its vision to provide a modular technological platform that allows open source companies to build content-related, knowledge-based applications for their customers. While aiming for a *high road* in terms of functionality, IKS is currently using industry-accepted technology such as OSGi, REST and RDF for implementation. We favour easy integration into existing frameworks and put emphasis on early and independent adoption of our software modules.

7.1 Introduction

In early 2008 a number of European ICT researchers gathered in Salzburg to discuss a project that should bring semantic technologies to small to medium firms that were active in the area of content management. Each of the participating researchers and their organisations had previously been involved in other such projects which had aimed at combining content management with intelligence of some sort and we felt that it was time for a rather ambitious endeavour that would require all parties to take a fresh look at what they had been doing in research as well as in business, up to that point.

The term *Interactive Knowledge Stack* really captures this ambition: forget about *content*—ask instead why this content is relevant to the user's current work at

---
Wernher Behrendt
IKS Project Manager, Salzburg Research, Salzburg, Austria, e-mail: `wernher.behrendt@salzburgresearch.at`

hand—in other words, what knowledge is conveyed by that content and for what purpose? Next, forget about *web usability* in a traditional sense—ask instead how the user would like to interact with the knowledge that is available to him, via the system? And finally, forget about one-shot, fragmented, *service-oriented* architecture and ask instead what set of fundamental machinery would be needed to form a minimal, yet powerful *Stack* for *Interaction* with *Knowledge* via web-based applications?

Researchers and senior developers are by no means united when it comes to answering the question whether CMS should tackle knowledge-based interaction with web-based digital content. This is particularly true for the IKS approach: why should anybody bother addressing such a complex theme that seems to repeat what some colleagues would consider to be *the old mistakes* of Artificial Intelligence?

Why is IKS not following the main ideas of *Semantic Web* as laid out by Tim Berners-Lee, in the late 1990s, leading to the well-known semantic web *Stack*? Why does IKS want to deviate from the ubiquitous interaction metaphor of web-search? There are plenty of CMSs out there, cheap and expensive, complex and simple, text-based, media-based, database-managed as you please, and there are superb search engines out there that find anything as long as it has a URL. Better even—or worse, for such an endeavour—the new ideas of cloud computing, map/reduce and Linked (open) Data are gaining widespread acceptance and so, there really seems no need for digging out *rule-based* systems, *expert systems* or *knowledge-based* systems and marrying them with CMSs. Could IKS be a fundamentally flawed idea? We beg to differ. We invite you in this chapter, to follow us on a journey that starts with database interoperation in the late 1970s, looks at the development of search as the prevailing metaphor for interaction on the web, and which offers a critical appraisal of semantic web technologies, leading to the conclusion that in our Gold rush to semantic web-based applications, we have left at home, some important inventions and engineering artefacts together with the manuals for them! Worse for the current semantic web, its foundation known as the Semantic Web (language) Layer Cake, is in fact, not a software stack—so who wants to build a CMS platform without clear architectural idea?

7.2 1970 to 1990: Relational Databases, Object-Orientation and AI

The period from 1970 to the early 1990s saw several research and technology strands that had profound effects on what the WWW is today. The early 1970s were characterised by attempts to formalise database technology. Bill Codd's relational model needed more than 10 years to come to fruition but since the mid-1980s, it has had the most profound impact on industry-strength database technology. Oracle, one of the largest IT-firms of today, was one of the first firms that offered a relational database system in the early 1980s.

From the late 1980s to the early 1990s, computer programming underwent a different but equally profound change from procedural programming to object-oriented design and implementation. At the more academic fringes of computing, Artificial Intelligence (AI) contributed successful search algorithms for knowledge domains such as Chess, and in the 1980s, Europe, Japan and the US started large-scale research programmes into fifth Generation Computing, with two distinct lines of work: US research was based on Lambda Calculus, functional programming and LISP as implementation language whereas Europe developed a strength in computational logic and developed the programming language Prolog on the basis of a pattern matching mechanism called unification. Many of these research-led programmes came to an end in the late 1980s and two new trends took over and managed to influence the computing industry: The first was object-oriented programming, claiming to be the best compromise between AI-type modelling and getting actual working software. This was the time of X-Windows for Unix-Workstations and also the time of the first Apple Macs. The other big trend was networked computing in local area networks, getting connected via wide-area networks—the early days of the Internet as we know it now, using the C Programming language in order to achieve networked computing based on sockets and ports, later to be followed by Remote Procedure Calls (RPC), Object Request Brokers (ORB), and even later, re-used in Service-oriented Architectures (SOA).

The networking technologies of the mid 1990s were fragmented to say the least: sockets, RPC, ORBs, yet different protocols for different DBMSs with prohibitively expensive business models, but soon ODBC and JDBC turned that market over by forcing the database vendors to follow the conventions of the application builders, rather than being able to impose their database network products on the customer.

And then, in 1992, came the WWW with HTTP and HTML. Within three years, the technological platforms of computing turned again, into a world of networked hypertext. From then on, computing went into phases of re-inventing many things again, but now taking the perspective of this networked world with people wanting to publish and exchange information, instead of just storing and retrieving it. As a consequence, the paradigm of working was beginning to change: from long-term systematic collecting of valuable resources, to gaining access *just in time* to different resources on demand, and immediately. At the turn of the Millennium, waiting for three weeks to obtain a copy of a paper from some remote library had become an unacceptable impediment to people's work.

7.3 1990 to 2000: From Altavista to Google – Post HOC Search Wins Over A Priori Structure

At the beginning of the 1990s, there were about 100 web servers on the planet and some forward looking research groups started to encode descriptions of their work in HTML and put them on those servers. For artificial intelligence (AI), for example, there were three or four servers for which one needed to know some entry points in order to get to the relevant AI pages. Only a couple of years later, every computing department had its own server and by the mid 1990s, the Web had moved from a departmental responsibility to the corporate marketing agenda. We were in the middle of the *dot.com* bubble. Knowing where to find things had become impossible and research departments had started an academic battle for the best search algorithms, partly sponsored by hardware makers who identified search on the web as a growth market for their big server machines. The precursor to Google started as one of these research projects, in the area of digital libraries, at Stanford University, in Spring 1996.[1]

The behaviour that we have all got accustomed to, since the mid 1990s, is that a-priori structures (e.g. database schemas) are difficult to maintain in chaotic and fast-growing data stores and that post-hoc ordering via indexing is a very good compromise for most users, most of the time. However, the question which percentage of VAT must be added when selling a luxury car in the UK in 2011 will not be answered precisely by your favourite search engine.

7.4 Critical Appraisal of the Search Metaphor in View of Content Management

Ever since the appearance of the AltaVista search engine in the mid-1990s our expectations and attitudes towards networked computing have changed: there were so many quick benefits available from searching the Web that we quickly changed our work patterns in order to reap these benefits.

However, everybody also paid a price in terms of interaction with knowledge: doctors writing prescriptions, electronics engineers developing integrated circuits, software engineers developing new applications and documenting them, or journalists gathering evidence for a news story they want to write. We have little difficulty in understanding that each of these jobs and the related tasks require specialist knowledge, completely different sets of information (aka content) and lead to very different kinds of outcomes or products. Despite all these easily graspable differences, we have developed the ubiquitous behaviour of LMGT4Y ("Let me google this for you!"). Let us look at the price we pay for letting a few large web content hosters control access to the most profound invention of the 21st Century (we place the automobile in the 20th Century and public transport in the 19th Century, for the purpose of simplification). Here are a few questions for your favourite web application and web access device:

- Ask your search engine for the current VAT rate on luxury cars, in the UK.
- Find the Facebook function which lets you list and download all your content (i.e. all the status lines you wrote and all the comments you wrote, and the images you uploaded).

---

[1] http://en.wikipedia.org/wiki/History_of_Google

- Still on Facebook—when you got your own texts back, then ask whether you can also have those texts and images to which your friends have given you access, e.g. those status lines on which you and others commented.
- Then ask your system for flights from Zurich to New York—this will work quite well—why?

The answer to the last question is roughly as follows: despite the fact that we are using a search engine for posing the question, we are actually being connected to a set of databases for a well defined item which has departure and arrival locations, dates of flights, and details of the providers and the prices charged. You get precise answers from systems that have a precise data structure and a precise query language. The search engine provider actually forces the data provider to return structured information. The same principle is used by Google for films and cinemas, and all the well-known social media platforms are moving to gathering their user data in ever more structured formats. Our conclusion is that the notion of well-defined data structure was never more alive than today, and that the reason for this is that any precise result is usually based on precise data! Let us explore this apparent contradiction between databases and web-based content retrieval.

7.5 Operating Systems, Web Communities and the Biggest CRM Database Ever Built

Many CMSs work by turning structured data from databases, into Google-able content in order for that content to become indexed and thus, act as an attractor for the defined business processes with which a web-based organisation supports its undertakings. They also add (mostly proprietary) structure in the form of metadata, to content, again in order to control and manage how web content is generated and presented to users. Part of their business model is to offer advanced features of search engine optimization (SEO): how to pre-configure your content so that it yields high rankings for search engines. In other words, while users get the simple search interface as the lowest common denominator (attractor), a sophisticated and complex set of defined structures is working in the background. Ever since the famous court cases against Microsoft's integration of the Internet Explorer into their operating system, the big players have been battling over this *new operating system for the Web*. Most of the smaller CMS providers are at best, passengers of the big players, by adopting their de facto standards, e.g. the emerging *Google Rich Snippets* formats.

The aforementioned battle for the operating system of the Web is not a technological issue: due to its history as a free and neutral resource, the Web Communities have developed an attitude and mind-set of *everything for free* or rather *no transfer of money*! As a result, the business models of the Web provide applications for free, information seekers pay no money (just like in free-TV), but they transfer information about themselves and others. The balance of power is clearly shifting towards those who run the web: for example, the previously free Scribd service (http://www.scribd.com/) now offers (November 2010) PDF downloads only to users of other platforms, notably Facebook and the user has to sign an online usage agreement where Scribd gets access to your Facebook friends information. What's happening? It is a one-way data-sucking campaign—from people to businesses. The big players are building the largest *customer relationship database* that the world has ever seen. However, this article is, now not going to discuss the social implications any further, we are just saying that IKS tries to give powerful technologies to small CMS providers so that neither they nor their customers, are completely at the mercy of the big players. IKS has a technological agenda that gives CMS providers and their customers more choice and independence as to how they want to manage their content. At the same time, IKS acknowledges the strengths of many of the *big* solutions and supports their use, too.

7.6 From Large Scale Customer Acquisition Engines to Business-Related Content Management

The traditional view on the WWW has been that this global knowledge space consists of documents. And as a result of that view, technologists have developed solutions that for a long time came from information retrieval and from the field of databases and data warehousing. There are now further trends that have begun to shape new solutions. Firstly, the growth of multimedia data (e.g. on Flickr or YouTube) has sparked R&D work in multimedia enabled search, image and video analysis, etc. Secondly, the growth in social media networks (LinkedIn, Facebook, Twitter, etc.) has made it increasingly interesting to bring back structured data, typically around the themes of *person, products, organisations, personal preferences* and similar issues. Thirdly, there is a new data wave approaching: as virtually every consumer item can now be connected and addressed via the Internet, we are faced with huge data streams and not enough system intelligence to cluster the large amounts of data into meaningful observations at a conceptual level. We are witnessing a development where all the dynamics of the real world are in some way or other, also represented as data clusters or data streams, in the virtual, networked world. Without needing a passport and visa, I can access information (or even, representations of real world events) that are located in some place outside my own geographic or socio-economic area. This ability brings us all closer (through our data traces), but at the same time, it begins to pose a political as well as a technological question of conscience: Cui bono?—Who will benefit from the new virtual world? Looking at developments over the past 30 years, we have moved from electronic customer cards at the local superstore, to a variety of web-based *free* services which seemingly give us great tools to work with, or services for leisure activities, and it is all based on a very simple financing model: *head count + detail of information = business value*, meaning that the more you find out about the unsuspecting user, the more value you generate, because you can better predict that user's behaviour as a consumer.

In January 2011, Facebook is rated at 50 Billion dollars, and claims to have 500 Million users. This means that the information they have about their average user is worth 100 dollars. Google, Facebook and other social networks must be seen as very large customer acquisition tools for themselves and potentially, for other companies. Since the cost of customer acquisition and subsequently, the lifetime value of customers have a high variance, this means in many cases that any new customer *bought* from Facebook at say, 10–100 dollars would be a worthwhile investment for the buying firms. Similarly, networks like Xing or LinkedIn get you closer to corporate customers so the premium for a customer there may be even higher. Unfortunately, there is only a small fraction of large companies who were able to carve up this new world very quickly, with such a simple business model. The second generation of successful web applications will need to be twice as smart for a tenth of the revenue and for providing a much more sophisticated service. Alternatively, they can try and change the rules of the game, e.g. by trying to influence legislation in such a way that the mammoth gathering of personal data gets stopped. We would argue that legislation in Europe and the US has missed the bus and that governments themselves are intrinsically on the data gatherers' side, usually in the name of *Homeland Security* or similar phrases. Again, we stop the discussion of the social implications here and ask simply: what does this mean for small-to-medium providers of CMSs? Are they already out of business or do they still stand a chance? Our answer is that they still stand a chance if they manage to either provide what the others do not want to provide, e.g. serious guarantees for privacy, or if they are smarter than the others in much smaller markets that require more sophisticated business models and knowledge about the nature of that business and thus, the nature of the customers. This is where we believe current semantic web research has not done all the necessary homework and where, as a result, the IKS agenda starts in a technical sense. Let us first explore the accomplishments and weaknesses of ten years of research in semantic web technology.

7.7 Critical Appraisal of the Semantic Web – We Need Technology Stacks, Not Language Cakes

This year (2011) is the tenth anniversary of the well-known *Semantic Web* article by Tim Berners-Lee, James Hendler and Ora Lassila (Berners-Lee et al., 2001). It had a simple, yet clear vision: A *knowledge representation language* (KRL) that is suitable for use in the Web, combined with actual knowledge encoded in ontologies, should be used by software agents, in order to deliver value for web customers. The formula was: *Semantic Web = Notation + Knowledge + Agents*. The next few years saw an academic battle for notations and KRLs, but little work on making the fundamental formula work, because most people and research groups shied away from the hardest part, which is combining any three elements (notation, knowledge, agents) into a working system. The only *architecture* that emerged was the semantic web language layer cake that was hotly debated (see for example [10]; [5]; [7]). As these and other discussions show, the semantic web kept suffering from at least three unresolved battles for academic supremacy: the battle for KRLs led to the semantically poor RDF and to the practically unsuitable OWL language families. The battle over formal semantics was heavily influenced by description logics, again at the expense of practical use on web-scale, whereas the battle for the most interesting part, namely agents, was left to semantic web services [2] which tried to resolve the problem by re-inventing everything and which ran out of steam after (mainly European) funding was exhausted. Neither the advanced approaches (semantic web services) nor the pragmatically oriented approaches (RDF-based, linked open data) are the kind of stuff that delivers on the promises of 2001, namely that smart web agents will help us solve practical problems via the web, e.g. by looking for a specialist doctor or for a nursery home for our elderly relative. Instead, we can subscribe to Google Health or similar software monocultures and for the price of our own privacy we can obtain such services from one of five or maybe a dozen providers worldwide. No intelligence in the sense of smart forms of reasoning over data via rules, no legally enforced privacy unless you accept US legislation as globally applicable, and just plain, large-scale data sucking. This is actually only part of the story: Again, we stop at this point with the socio-economic and political discussion, and reduce the issue to its technological and scientific problems.

Scientifically, any KRL for the web should, in principle, be capable of describing processes and objects, i.e. be able to represent world knowledge in a dynamic and in a static fashion. Another requirement is that it needs to effortlessly move between levels of granularity and abstraction. This brings any such language close to natural language. While we can still try to remain strictly formal for a computer-processable language, we do require the language to be generative. That is, it must be possible to construct new meaning with a mix of syntactic means and with lexical semantics, i.e. preferably combining existing words or, occasionally, introducing new words that follow the syntactic rules and allow us to convey new meanings. This is known as compositional semantics. With such a language, we will be able to describe real-world phenomena, in a machine-processable way. Note that content management is management of information that represents something in the real world worth managing. To the people who buy a CMS, that content means something and the business model of a CMS provider should be based on understanding what that content means to the customer. Then one can find a sweet spot where a CMS provider delivers best service for a reasonable price. This is why the question of knowledge representation must matter to CMS: because it determines the way in which you can manage your customer's content. RDF is semantically poor, but it is the only notation that is universally accepted and it gives us one fundamental capability: we can convey meaning through a little bit of structure and through lots of lexical semantics. In other words, if we ever invent a better KRL, then lifting existing information from RDF to the new KRL will be at least easier than moving it from plain XML or HTML to such a new language. Thus, we do not lose by using RDF, although we could gain if we had something better.

The original vision of the semantic web was very much in line with a fundamental observation that has been ascribed to Edsgar Dijkstra: *Computing = data structures + algorithms*. Note that Dijkstra ignored the issue of *language* and *notation*, which he rightly assumed as an a-priori for any symbolic processing. So, leaving aside notation and syntax we are left with the semantic web formula consisting of lexical semantics in the form of ontologies and agents as algorithms that handle them. And in the same way in which algorithms and data structures form an eco-system (preferably one with mathematical properties such as lambda calculus or relational algebra), any ontology needs its own algorithms or—if you prefer the term—its software agents that can handle and interpret expressions based on the ontology. This now means that any semantic processing system (e.g. a working CMS) must declare its notations, its knowledge models (ontologies) and it must offer its algorithms that will do useful things with the knowledge models.

It is comforting for the researchers in IKS, to see that in January 2011, one of the great evangelists of the semantic web, James Hendler, resurrects much of that original view by focusing his own research agenda on three themes [8]. Hendler identifies as his research interests firstly the large-scale, linked data challenge phrasing it as "providing some firmer basis for large-scale representation and reasoning"; secondly he wonders how we can get order into the emerging large amounts of governmental data sets and what the actual benefits will be, of making them available. Hendler's third and final research objective is "Relevate the Agents to Semantic Web connection". We interpret this as acknowledging that after ten years of research, the third variable of the Semantic Web equation is still unbound, and the evidence for the second variable (ontologies) being bound, is still scarce.

The conclusion from the critical appraisal of semantic web technology is that the cake of language layers is not useful for CMS providers nor for anybody who needs to create a working semantic system in less than one year, to satisfy a customer's web content management demand. The sobering fact is that there is no actual semantic technology stack that is approaching any level of industrial maturity—at least not for CMS technology. Additionally, the paradigmatic differences in implementation technologies inside the semantic web (e.g. RDF versus OWL) and outside the semantic web communities (e.g. relational databases versus triple stores) are still huge barriers against widespread adoption.

7.8 Strategic Positioning and Main Elements of IKS

Our starting point was that many organisations already have CMSs, ranging from corporate document management to global web content management. Some CMS providers have even got close relationships with eBusiness system providers. In other words, CMS providers often have a *foot in the door* when it comes to their customer base and they may be in a position to extend their business by adding services to their current portfolio. At the same time, there is a danger particularly for SMEs that their technology base is becoming inadequate. This is due to the fact that many

CMS started off as simple aggregations of web-management functionality, quickly built upon the so-called LAMP Stack (Linux, Apache, mySQL, PHP). These smaller organisations cannot handle a complete system overhaul and significant R&D unless they get some assistance from outside. IKS is an attempt to redress the economic balance again, in order to give customers more choice by keeping more technology players in the game. Better even, if those technology players get additional tools in order to access more niche markets with well-suited solutions then the danger of content-monopolies or customer-access monopolies can be abated to some degree. We therefore designed the IKS technology project as follows:

- It is addressed primarily at European SME CMS technology providers
- It delivers software components which are organised as a well-defined technology stack
- It focuses on functionality which enables knowledge-based interaction with content
- It does not advocate *semantic web technology* per se, but focuses on utility gained from enhancing existing CMSs with *semantic features*
- It contributes to moving from *one-of-a-kind* design to a reference architecture as a means of fostering standardisation and governance within the CMS industry
- It uses RESTful services as a safe way of ensuring integration with existing CMSs
- It uses a strict, BSD-based open source approach to ensure re-use without constraints

7.8.1 Addressing CMS Providers

In the course of the project, IKS has approached several dozens European SME, CMS providers many of whom are willing to become *early adopters* of IKS technology. The Early Adopters receive an initial small grant through which their lead developers can get to know the ideas and the existing software prototypes. Subsequently, the CMS providers can themselves, take part in the open source process wherever they feel it is worth doing so.

7.8.2 The Interactive Knowledge Stack (IKS)

IKS had originally eight layers. For ease of communication we collapsed them into a simpler, four-layer model [1, cf. Table 1]. At the top is user interaction and knowledge presentation, below the interaction layer is the knowledge representation layer consisting of static (structural) and dynamic (process-related) knowledge. The third layer encompasses all issues of distribution and interoperation. The fourth, bottom-layer of the model deals with persistence and with the issue of what constitutes a knowledge entity in the target system.

The first four columns of Table 1 represent the developer's and the customizer's requirements for an IKS-type system: the software engineer develops a new module and registers it—this is mostly functionality already provided by OSGi. When a system is tailored to the needs of a specific customer organisation, certain modules will get activated and—depending on what was foreseen by the developer—specific modules may get customised according to the end user needs. These four capabilities comprise the functionality of the Alpha Stack.

The last four columns of the table address the functionality that we expect to be available for the end user, at each layer of the Stack. The logic of this conceptualisation follows a simplified content life-cycle: content is first created by some author; once it is created, it can be queried by other users; querying means simply getting relevant content back, but typically that content is further formatted, manipulated, filtered or aggregated and these types of further processing are subsumed as *consuming content*. The most advanced form of processing query results is to make them available for further manipulation by the user—the user is then able to interact with the content.

In the methodology of IKS, each developer needs to address this matrix and decide what it means for the functionality he is trying to provide. For example, the developer has to ask himself: "am I building something that is for the backend or does my component have implications for the front-end where the final content consumer is situated?" The top four layers provide a *semantic interaction framework* which gives the developer not only guidance, but is designed to also return semantically annotated content if the developer chooses to employ the framework. This is an example where methodical design gives us *semantics for free* when the system is deployed.

7.8.3 Knowledge-based Interaction with Content

Managing *content* is, unfortunately, synonymous with an admission that those who deal with the content do not know and do not even want to know, what the content is about. As soon as we do know something about the content, we are entering the world of *knowledge* management systems, and as soon as we try to model the environment in which this knowledge lives, we have entered the world of *knowledge-based systems*. IKS is an overt attempt to move from a (knowledge-ignorant) content view to a (content-aware) knowledge view on content management. The reasoning behind it is that ultimately, all content will get generated from more or less sophisticated knowledge representations. The challenge for developers will then be how they can build applications that generate the right kind of content at the right time, from the right data and from formally encoded knowledge about the data. The health sector provides us with good examples. For example, a patient health record containing information about visits to the hospital, x-rays, MRI pictures and specialist's diagnoses is a highly structured piece of time-based knowledge. If the patient has a chronic disease then the diagnoses, prescriptions and lab-results tell a very detailed story of that patient's quality of life. If the task of managing health records was given to a traditional CMS, most of the interesting, meaningful information would simply not be *picked up* by the system, because its level of abstraction essentially reduces to

<patient> – <has-content-item> – <diagnosis>

whereas the doctor's level of abstraction would be

<patient> – <suffers-from> – <chronic-lymphatic-leucemia> – <at> – <date>

Note that both abstractions refer to the same *document*. Note that, of course, finding the document for the patient is possible in both levels of abstraction. However, the issue of managing explicit semantics becomes a serious issue if that patient is allergic to certain anaesthetics and the patient record system can only offer

<diagnosis> but cannot offer <patient> – <is-susceptible-to> – <allergic-reaction-of-type>

Interactive Knowledge means that our content must be accessible at the level abstraction that our end users need for their work. In the case of allergic reactions this is a safety critical issue and therefore easy to understand, but we are also interested in the many issues that are not safety-critical, but make systems simply smarter to work with. For the system to *understand* the application domain at some reasonable level of abstraction is the objective of IKS.

7.8.4 Technologies for Semantic Content Management

The notion of *understanding* content brings us to a technology that became a hype in 2001 when Berners-Lee, Hendler and Lassila published an article in Scientific American, about their vision of the *Semantic Web* where they gave similarly compelling examples of future uses for the web as the ones described above. The word *semantics* has, ironically, become somewhat void in its meaning since then, because the core technologies of the semantic web do not fit together in a reasonable technology stack. It is for this reason that IKS decided to start with RESTful services that allow developers to decouple *semantic* functionality from *technology choice* [9]. For example, if a CMS provider has put several dozen person-years into a JCR-based storage solution and has developed good user-functionality on top of that then it is simply not viable to say: "you must switch to RDF-based triple-stores before you can use our ontology-based semantic system!" However, it is perfectly reasonable to offer a RESTful service that utilises some RDF-based reasoning component and is then able to feed the results back into the CMS provider's technology stack.

7.8.5 A Reference Architecture for IKS

When we analysed the systems of the CMS providers we noticed big differences in the architectural diagrams they were using. Thanks to the abstractions introduced by our researchers from the software engineering field [3], we were able to relate the diagrams to each other, and we were able to produce a first reference architecture for IKS as shown in Fig. 7.1. This makes it now possible for CMS providers to *rationally reconstruct* their own systems at a conceptual level and thus, decide how to best augment their own systems with semantic functionalities offered by IKS software components.

7.8.6 RESTful Services for Integration with Existing CMS

Building a reference implementation for the whole stack can be done either in full or as a *lightweight* Stack. A full implementation would amount to building a complete CMS from scratch, i.e. starting with a green field. This has of course, much academic appeal, but is not likely to have impact in the face of mature full CMS that offer rich user functionality. IKS has opted for a mixed approach that also reflects the limited resources available. Our design emphasises in the first instance, quick connectivity with existing systems and we therefore agreed to industry's request for the use of RESTful services.

7.8.7 BSD-based Open Source Approach to Ensure Re-use without Constraints

The most recent development in IKS has been the move of the code base to an Apache incubation process [4]. This new version of IKS is taking the more mature research components of the Stack to make them available to a wider community of developers. A major decision was to keep licensing very permissive, i.e. accepting not only the BSD-style licensing scheme, but also accepting the rules of the Apache Foundation when it comes to representation of the project. That is, letting developers act as independent individuals, which can occasionally cause tensions between the *corporate* interests of the project and the actual development in Apache which is based on a developer-centred meritocracy.

7.9 Conclusion – Research Follows Industry in the Interest of Impact

It is worth noting that IKS took a different route from many other semantic technology projects with respect to the basic framework underpinning the work. Following a lengthy requirements phase, we became almost paralysed by a discussion of research-led frameworks, tools and technologies: should we build large-scale ontologies in Protege or other ontology building and management tools? Should we

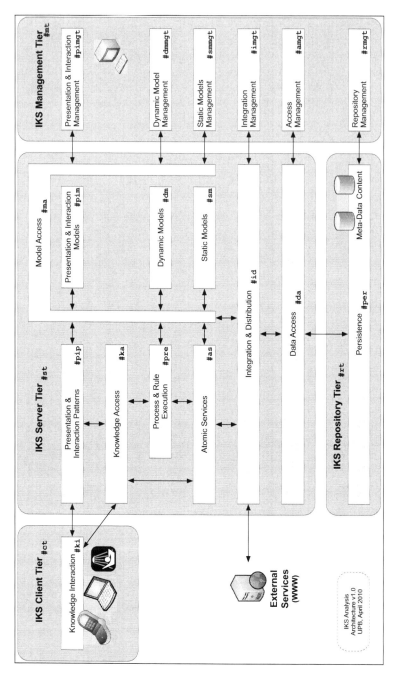

Fig. 7.1: The IKS reference architecture

use this triple store or another? Should we use meta-models to make the research prototypes interoperable with each other? Then, some of the senior developers from industry made it clear that they were neither happy with the discussion nor with the available choices. The break-through came at a developers' workshop in early 2010 when—led by two senior industrial developers—the team built a first prototype system within a few days, using OSGi and some conventions for RESTful services. RDF is at present the only semantic web technology that is being used in IKS, for encoding knowledge items and for information exchange [11]. The focus of that first system was on semantic enhancements for primarily text-based content items.

One of the continuing challenges of IKS is to avoid being frightened by the capabilities of the big players as well as avoiding to try and beat them at their own game. Our first prototype, the FISE system was the result of carefully negotiating these dangers. FISE manages a collection of semantic enhancement engines that can be used to improve existing collections of documents by adding semantic structure in a step-by-step fashion [6]. IKS seems to be placed in a good window of opportunity: the big players are increasingly using sophisticated data structures in order to improve their tools for gathering marketing intelligence about their customers. At the same time, governments are being pushed to open up their data vaults for Linked Data. The web is growing in depth, because it is becoming the digital, holographic mirror of human activity. With the web becoming the communication infrastructure of the world, there will be lots and lots more *content* to manage, and managing it well will mean distinguishing one kind of content from another kind of content. The *Interactive Knowledge Stack* should provide helpful technologies for managing these many types of content for their many kinds of uses. Remember: talking of *content* is the admission of not knowing what exactly, we are interacting with!

References

1. Behrendt, W.: The design vision for developing the interactive knowledge stack (2010). URL http://wiki.iks-project.eu/index.php/File:IKS_Stack_Design_Vision_2010_06_02_wernher_behrendt.pdf
2. Cardoso, J., Sheth, A. (eds.): Semantic Web Services, Processes and Applications. Springer: Heidelberg, Germany (2006)
3. Christ, F., Daga, E., Engels, G., Germesin, S., Kilic, O., Nagel, B., Sauer, S.: Iks deliverable on architecture (2010). URL http://wiki.iks-project.eu/index.php/IKS_Alpha_Development
4. Delacretaz, B.: Apache stanbol (2010). URL http://incubator.apache.org/stanbol/
5. Gerber, A., van der Merwe, A.J. & Barnard, A.: A Functional Semantic Web Architecture. In Proceedings of the 5th European Semantic Web Conference (ESWC'08), Tenerife, Spain (2008)
6. Grisel, O.: Introducing FISE, the Open Source RESTful Semantic Engine (2010). URL http://blogs.nuxeo.com/dev/2010/08/introducing-fise-the-restful-semantic-engine.html
7. Hendler, J.: My take on the layer cake (2009). URL http://www.cs.rpi.edu/~hendler/presentations/LayercakeDagstuhl-share.pdf
8. Hendler, J.: Semantic Web New Year's Resolutions (2011). URL http://blogs.nature.com/jhendler/2011/01/03/semantic-web-new-years-resolutions

9. NORD Software Consulting: RESTful Services, Classification of HTTP-based APIs (2010). URL http://nordsc.com/ext/classification_of_http_based_apis.html
10. Patel-Schneider, P.F.: A revised architecture for semantic web reasoning. In: F. Fages, S. Soliman (eds.) Principles and Practice of Semantic Web Reasoning, pp. 32–36. Springer, Heidelberg, Germany (2005)
11. W3C: RDF Current Status (2010). URL http://www.w3.org/standards/techs/rdf#w3c_all

Biographical Notes

Wernher Behrendt holds an MSc in Geography and English (Graz, Austria) and an MSc in Cognitive Science (Manchester, UK). He worked as Research Associate in the Informatics Department at Rutherford Appleton Laboratory near Oxford (1990–1994) and as Senior Research Associate in the field of database interoperation at the University of Cardiff (1995-1998). After a year in Germany, he took up a position as Senior Researcher at Salzburg Research where he became Head of the Knowledge-Based Information Systems group in 2003. He led RTD projects in the 5th and 6th framework programme and was lead author of a study for the European Commission in 2003, on the future of electronic publishing. Since the beginning of 2009, he is coordinator and principal investigator of the Integrated Project IKS. He likes endangered species of all sorts, and so it is not surprising that his favourite programming language is Prolog.

Chapter 8
Essential Requirements for Semantic CMS

Valentina Presutti

Abstract CMS have to support a set of essential requirements in order to upgrade to semantic CMS. They have to own the capability of lifting content and enrich it with data from external, semantic sources such as the LOD cloud. They have to handle ontologies and rules, share and reuse ontology patterns, and are able to convert legacy data to RDF as well as to transform RDF data according to different ontologies. They have to perform automatic reasoning for inferring new knowledge from the existing one, scope this reasoning to a specific task, and finally store triples in a knowledge base by keeping them connected to related content items. We derive these requirements through a simple scenario in which a CMS user wants to enrich content with external data after checking the integrity of them according to personalized validity rules. Finally, we briefly describe KReS, a set of software components implementing the essential requirements for knowledge representation and reasoning support in a CMS.

8.1 Introduction

Content Management Systems (CMS) play a key role in the publishing of content on the web. On one hand they are the main supporting tools for users who create and curate web content, on the other hand they allow for encoding and publishing such content on the web i.e. according to web standard formats. CMS can benefit from semantic web technologies for both aspects and upgrade to so called *semantic* CMS (sCMS).

In our view, a sCMS features technologies that enable the minimization of the amount of business logic, domain knowledge, and related reasoning that needs to be "hard coded" in CMS software, i.e. knowledge—specific for a system and a

---

Valentina Presutti
Researcher, Semantic Technology Laboratory of the National Research Council (ISTC-CNR), Rome, Italy, e-mail: valentina.presutti@cnr.it

domain—that is directly expressed as software code. Semantic technologies enable to maximize the CMS software capability to adapt in different contexts through the exploitation of semantic descriptions. As a ultimate goal, a sCMS aims at lowering the cognitive load of its users when they perform knowledge-intensive tasks. The Interactive Knowledge Stack (IKS) project (http://iks-project.eu) has the aim of developing a software framework and associated conceptual architecture and methodology good practices for enabling CMS vendors and developers to perform a smooth upgrade of their CMS to sCMS. Behrendt (in this book) describes the overall vision and approach of IKS.

Figure 8.1 depicts the envisioned IKS architecture of a sCMS. The stack describes a number of layers that should communicate to each other in order to allow users of a CMS to interact with knowledge as opposed to interacting with mere information. The intuition behind the last sentence is that the stack, through the exploitation of semantic technologies, is able to support users in performing knowledge-intensive work better than traditional information retrieval-based systems. The difference lays in the capability of the stack to reduce the effort that users put in processing all information in order to select, and then handle those that are relevant to address their task. For example, in the process of writing magazine news, the author might want to search for related articles, and other information about the entities mentioned in the article. She will have to understand, from a huge number of results, which ones are relevant to the topic of her article according to specific criteria (which could be different from popularity). She might want to identify content that can be directly reused or referred to, and semantic descriptions from the web about e.g. people, mentioned in the article and reuse them for enhancing the article content, etc. The idea of IKS is to support such activities by e.g. identifying relevant content, providing useful recommendations and explanations, choosing the most suitable presentation, etc.

In IKS, our approach for analyzing requirements has been based on user stories provided by CMS providers as well as on the need of pushing the state of the art of CMS systems and semantic technologies in general. The reader can refer to the Work Package 3 deliverables of the IKS project [18] and [10] for a comprehensive report on the analysis of requirements of the IKS framework.

An important aspect of our work has been to guarantee that the developed components and services would have been reusable by potentially every CMS. We had to imagine a software framework, independent on any CMS platform, and able to potentially support every CMS developer in building semantic applications and functionalities. We committed to modularity, portability, and reusability of components. We started the implementation based on a prioritization of the identified requirements, and developed a number of demonstrators base on scenarios for proving the effectiveness of the IKS software developed so far.

The focus of this chapter is on the stack layers that are in charge of supporting knowledge representation and reasoning capabilities of the stack through the adoption of semantic web technologies. The experience of developing IKS demonstrators taught us what are the *essential features*, *hence requirements* that distinguish a traditional CMS from a sCMS. We present them in this work with the help a sample

8 Essential Requirements for Semantic CMS

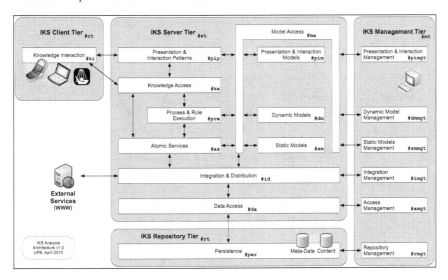

Fig. 8.1: The Interactive Knowledge Stack architecture

scenario, and conducting the analysis from the perspective of sCMS users, being they authors, editors, administrators, or developers.

In summary, a sCMS is able to process and produce semantic content in the form of *RDF data*—RDF [14] is the semantic web standard language for representing information about resources in the web. Such data have to be organized by means of *ontologies*, expressed in OWL [20]—the standard language for web ontologies—and possibly governed by additional *logic rules* e.g. based on SWRL [16] have to be accompanied by the ability of performing *automatic reasoning* over the data to the aim of enriching the CMS knowledge base. An important feature of a sCMS is data transformation. *Transformation of conceptual schemas*, and their enhancement to OWL ontologies or RDF vocabularies enables interoperability with legacy systems, and with external sources. *Transformation of RDF data* represented with a vocabulary to RDF data based on another vocabulary improves interoperability with other semantic applications. Finally, a sCMS provides features for *exploiting/reusing linked data* [4]—external semantic content present on the web, such as the Linking Open Data (LOD) cloud [21]—as well as contributing to it e.g. by producing automatic annotation in RDFa [3].

The rest of the chapter is organized as follows. Next, essential requirements for CMS from the perspective of the Semantic Web are discussed. Then, KReS, a suite of components for Knowledge Representation and Reasoning Support, is presented. Afterwards, related work is described. Finally, we conclude this chapter with a short summary.

8.2 Semantic Web Essential Requirements for CMS

In order to explain the rationale behind the identification of the essential requirements for a sCMS, we refer to a sample scenario, which has been defined during discussions with CMS providers participating in the IKS consortium. Based on this scenario we identify requirements for three main actors of a sCMS: the author/editor (typically who creates and publishes content), the administrator (who configures and customizes the CMS functionalities), and the developer (who implements functionalities in a specific CMS platform). From the use cases identified for the three actors we deduce the set of essential requirement that are needed for upgrading a CMS to sCMS. Such essential requirements are general with respect to the scenario i.e. they enable the development of additional scenarios that rely on semantic capabilities of a CMS.

8.2.1 Integrity Check of External Data: A Scenario for Semantic CMS

In the process of creating content, a desirable functionality would be that of retrieving relevant related semantic web entities, and associating parts of the text to them. For example, if a journalist would write a magazine article on Michael Jackson, the sCMS would recommend as related content, the DBPedia (http://dbpedia.org/) resources which refer to the person "Michael Jackson", and possible other relevant web entities e.g. of the LOD cloud. The author might want to gather all the semantic information about those entities, store them in her CMS knowledge base, and exploit them for providing enriched descriptions. For example, an info-box about Michael Jackson would include information about his birth date and city, pictures, etc. Before such external knowledge is integrated within her CMS knowledge base, the author might want to check the integrity of the gathered data against some validity rules. For example, she might want to integrate data about persons only if they include a name, a place of birth, and a picture.

Figure 8.2 shows a UML Use Case diagram detailing the functionalities identified by the analysis of the scenario.

Author/Editor use cases

Once the sCMS has processed the text written by an author, it identifies a number of LOD entities and presents them to her. The following list describes the use cases from the perspective of an author performing the integrity check scenario with a sCMS.

8 Essential Requirements for Semantic CMS 95

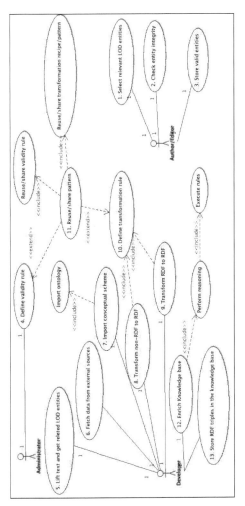

Fig. 8.2: UML Use Case diagram for the integrity check for external sources scenario. It shows the functionalities needed for realizing the scenario from the perspective of three main actors: the author/editor of CMS content, the Administrator of a semantic CMS, the Developer of a semantic CMS.

1. **Select relevant LOD entities**: the sCMS identifies a set of LOD entities in some way related to the content created by an author[1], and present them to her. The author selects the ones that she intends to inspect to the aim of enriching the created content, and the sCMS knowledge base.

---

[1] The criteria by which the entities are retrieved can be different; various approaches are implemented by a number of FISEs as described by Delacretaz and Marth (in this book).

2. **Check entity integrity**: the selected LOD entities, together with their semantic descriptions—their associated RDF graph of property values—are validated against a set of rules that define the conditions for integrity of data in that specific context. Such integrity rules are defined as part of the sCMS configuration activity (hence by administrators). A possible extension of this requirement would include the possibility for authors of defining new personalized (local) integrity rules.
3. **Store valid entities**: all or part of the entities that positively passed the integrity check can be stored in the sCMS knowledge base for future use.

Figure 8.3 depicts how words in a sCMS editor can be associated to LOD entities related to them. In this example, the system recognizes four DBPedia[2] entities (referring to two persons and two places).

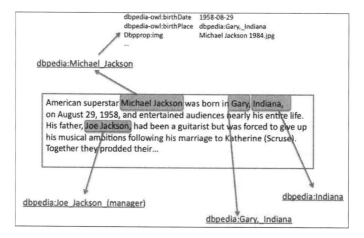

Fig. 8.3: A text created by an author/editor and the related LOD entities detected by a sCMS.

Administrator use cases

In order to enable the integrity check feature the sCMS should include, in its configuration settings, a set of validity rules. Such settings impact on the whole sCMS configuration, hence they are part of the activities typically performed by who has administrator access rights in the system.

4. **Define validity rule**: the administrator of a sCMS defines a set of rules for configuring the integrity check function. When the integrity check is run, the selected

---

[2] The prefix dbpedia: stands for http://dbpedia.org/page

entities e.g. from LOD, are validated against these rules. Only the ones that positively passed the check can be stored in the sCMS knowledge base, and used for enhancing the associated content.

5. **Reuse/share patterns (Reuse/share validity rules)**: the sCMS provides access to a repository of ontology patterns [6]. Validity rules are a special type of ontology patterns. The administrator can both store the defined rules for future use, and reuse existing rules possibly defined by other administrators. Furthermore, such repository should have both a local and a public view. The local view is only accessible by the administrator of the specific sCMS, while the public view is connected to a network of other repositories, where rules are shared among sCMS providers, and users. This use case requires the usage of a shared language for defining rules—which in the semantic web context could be the core dialect of the W3C Recommendation Rule Interchange Format (RIF) [5]. It also supports interoperability between different sCMS, and the spreading of good and common practices. Figure 8.4 (a) shows an example of validity rule expressed in KReS syntax[3]. The rule can be read as follows: everything that is a person, and has a name, and has a homepage is a valid content.

Developer use cases

The following use cases identify functionalities, as they would be described from a developer perspective, if she specified ready-to-use functionalities of a software framework—that can be integrated with potentially any CMS platform—that supports the development of this scenario.

6. **Lift text and get related LOD entities**: in this context, with the term "lifting" we refer to the process of associating some content with new data. Such data enhance the original content by adding semantic information expressed in a machine-readable form that can be processed by other applications. In this scenario the lifting of text consists of associating words in natural language with related LOD entities (as depicted in Fig. 8.3), and express this association in RDF. For example, the term "Sony" in a text would be associated with e.g. the DBPedia entity http://dbpedia.org/page/Sony. The way the text lifting is performed can rely on various techniques such as information extraction and Natural Language Processing (NLP) tools. Details on techniques used to this aim are described in [9]. In IKS this feature is handled by the lifting layer and implemented through so called FISEs[4], as described by Delacretaz and Marth in this book. In few words, FISE is a OSGi-based RESTful engine that enhances text through pluggable engines that perform some lifting process.

---

[3] KReS syntax is the language used in the KReS framework (see KReS Section 8.3) for expressing rules. Notes about KReS syntax can be found at http://stlab.istc.cnr.it/stlab/KReS/KReSRuleLanguage

[4] http://wiki.iks-project.eu/index.php/FISE

```
                    Only Person with name and homepage

              dbpedia = <http://dbpedia.org/ontology/> .
              foaf=http://xmlns.com/foaf/0.1/.
              ruleIntegrity[is(dbpedia:Person, ?x) .
              has(foaf:name, ?x, ?y) .
              has(foaf:homepage, ?x, ?z)
              -> is(dbpedia:ValidContent, ?x)]

                                (a)
```

```
                       DBPedia Person -> Google Person
peopleTypeRule [ is(dbpedia:Person, ?x) -> is(google:Person, ?x) ] .
peopleNameRule [ is(dbpedia:Person, ?x) . values(foaf:name, ?x, ?y) -> values(google:name, ?x, ?y) ] .
peopleNickRule [ is(dbpedia:Person, ?x) . values(foaf:nick, ?x, ?y) -> values(google:nickname, ?x, ?y) ] .
peoplePhotoRule [ is(dbpedia:Person, ?x) . has(dbpedia:thumbnail, ?x, ?y) -> has(google:photo, ?x, ?y) ] .
peopleProfessionRule [ is(dbpedia:Person, ?x) . has(dbpedia:profession, ?x, ?y) -> has(google:title, ?x, ?y) ] .
peopleRoleRule [ is(dbpedia:Person, ?x) . values(dbpedia:role, ?x, ?y) -> values(google:role, ?x, ?y) ] .
peopleHomepageRule [ is(dbpedia:Person, ?x) . has(foaf:homepage, ?x, ?y) -> has(google:url, ?x, ?y) ] .
peopleAffiliationRule [ is(dbpedia:Person, ?x) . has(dbpedia:employer, ?x, ?y) -> has(google:affiliation, ?x, ?y) ] .
peopleKnowsRule [ is(dbpedia:Person, ?x) . has(foaf:knows, ?x, ?y) -> has(google:friend, ?x, ?y) ] .
peopleAddressRule [ is(dbpedia:Person, ?x) . values(dbpedia:address, ?x, ?y) -> values(google:address, ?x, ?y) ] .
                                (b)
```

Fig. 8.4: Examples of rules expressed in KReS syntax. (a) An example of validity rule expressing that valid content are entities of type person, with a name and a homepage. (b) An example of transformation recipe (a set of transformation rules) for converting RDF data about people represented with the DBPedia ontology to RDF data about people represented with the Google Rich Snippet vocabulary.

7. **Fetch data from external sources**: semantic entities related to a certain content item, e.g. LOD entities related to a news, are possibly associated with additional semantic descriptions e.g. RDF graphs from the web of data. The RDF graph of related entities has to be gathered from the LOD cloud, and made available to the sCMS for further computation.
8. **Import conceptual scheme (Import ontology)**: a specific instance of a sCMS typically supports an organization working in a given business domain. In order to classify and manage content items, each organization relies on conceptual schemes that are either standards or have been ad-hoc developed for their business purposes e.g. a taxonomy that defines content item types. A sCMS has to provide features for importing such conceptual schemes in its knowledge base, and use them in semantic processes that it performs. This functionality contributes to guarantee the compatibility of a sCMS with legacy resources. This functionality also includes importing OWL ontologies and RDF vocabularies.
9. **Transform non-RDF to RDF**: with the assumption that a sCMS supports semantic web standards, and exploits them in order to perform semantic processes, it has to support the conversion of legacy structured data to RDF data. The aim of this functionality is to homogenize the format used for representing semantic

data within the sCMS for enabling automatic computations. For example, it has to be possible to convert an XSD taxonomy used by a business organization to a RDF vocabulary (or OWL ontology). IKS software support to this functionality consists of a tool that allows to plug-in software components that embed the criteria for transforming data representation formats to RDF. Built-in plug-ins support relational databases and XSD/XML (see KReS Section 8.3).

10. **Transform RDF to RDF**: this functionality allows refactoring RDF data. RDF refactoring includes the case of transforming the data according to a vocabulary or ontology different from the one currently used. For example, in order to produce Google rich snippets [7] for a certain web page, the RDF data associated with that page has to be represented based on the Google Rich Snippet vocabulary, while in order to index the same page according to a taxonomy of subjects external RDF data associated with that page has to be represented based on e.g. Simple Knowledge Organisation System (SKOS) [15]. In this scenario, a user may want to check the integrity of data according to ontologies and rules, which are different from the ones originally used for representing the data e.g. defining validity rules based on a proprietary vocabulary and apply them to DBPedia data.

11. **Define transformation rules**: the previous use case i.e. RDF refactoring, relies on the definition of transformation rules (also called mapping rules). The transformation rules can be either hard-coded in software plugins (similar to what happens for the non-RDF to RDF transformations), or defined with a standard language, and processed by a component able to execute them. The solution adopted by IKS for RDF refactoring is the most flexible one (as described in the KReS Section 8.3), it allows developers to define and execute customized transformation rules. Figure 8.4 (b) shows an example of transformation rules expressed in KReS syntax. By executing them on a set of DBPedia data about people, we would obtain a set of data about people represented with the Google vocabulary.

12. **Reuse/share patterns (Reuse/share transformation recipe/pattern)**: transformation rules are a special type of ontology patterns as well as validity rules, hence they can be stored for future use, and shared among the sCMS community of developers. For this reason, the integration with a repository of transformation rules with both local and public views (see Reuse/share pattern use case from the Administrator perspective) is a desirable feature of a sCMS. Consider the example given in Fig. 8.3 (b) that set of rules can be reused by anybody who wants to automatically produce Google rich snippets for people.

13. **Enrich knowledge base (Perform reasoning/Execute rules)**: one of the benefits deriving from semantic technologies is the possibility to infer new knowledge from the existing one so as to enrich the sCMS knowledge base. With reference to the integrity check scenario, there are at least two possible ways of enriching the sCMS knowledge base. First, by simply storing the data gathered from external sources (RDF triples) and positively validated. Second, the ontologies (and associated rules) used for representing the data can be exploited for inferring new knowledge, and store all of part of it in the sCMS knowledge base. In order to infer new knowledge based on ontology axioms and logic rules, a sCMS needs

reasoning capabilities, hence the support for integrating OWL reasoning components. Reasoning is a complex and time-consuming task, which could impact on the performances of the sCMS. Furthermore, a developer might want to perform only certain reasoning operations, and contextualize them to a subset of the data, a subpart of the sCMS ontology network, or a subset of the rules defined in the system. In other words, a sCMS should be able to perform contextualized inferences, where the context refers to specific task, dataset, ontologies, rules that could be a subset of those loaded by the whole sCMS environment.

14. **Store RDF triples in the knowledge base**: the semantic data, in the form of RDF triples, have to be stored in the knowledge base. This implies the need of integrating the CMS with a triple store, and of keeping the connection with the related content items.

Essential Requirements of a sCMS

From the use cases above we derive a set of requirements, capabilities that a sCMS has to feature in order to support semantically enhanced functionalities. While the perspective of author/editor and administrator lead us to the identification of use cases, which are tailored to the particular scenario i.e. integrity check of external data, the perspective of the developer gives us a view on essential functionalities of a sCMS that are required in many other cases. They are summarized as follows:

1. **Content lifting and enrichment**: the capability to enrich content items with entities that have a URI in the web of data i.e. linked data. In other words it is the capability to apply information extraction and NLP techniques in order to identify key entities of a content item, match them with semantic entities on the web e.g. LOD entities, and enrich the content item with structured data that explicitly represent such enhancement so as to make other applications able to process it e.g. in RDF [9].
2. **Exploitation of semantic web resources**: the capability of interoperate with external sources e.g., the LOD cloud, RSS feeds, microformats, etc. for retrieving descriptions e.g. fetching the RDF descriptive graph of a semantic web resource, to be exploited for content enrichment.
3. **Data reengineering and refactoring to semantic web standards**: the capability to convert non-RDF to RDF data, and of transforming RDF data according to different ontologies/vocabularies.
4. **Ontology and rule management**: the capability to handle ontologies and rules i.e. defining and managing ontologies and logic rules.
5. **Sharing and reuse of ontology patterns**: the capability to share and reuse ontologies and rules that have been defined for addressing specific tasks.
6. **Scope-based reasoning**: the capability of inferring new knowledge on the basis of ontology axioms and rules. The complexity of reasoning in a sCMS should be minimized according to the need of specific tasks. In order to obtain this behavior, the management of ontologies and rules should be contextualized in a

task-oriented way so as to execute reasoning based only on the set of ontologies and rules that are required for that specific task. In this way regardless the set of ontologies and rules used by the whole sCMS, only those in the scope of a specific task are processed when performing automated reasoning for executing that task.
7. **Triple storage**: the capability of storing RDF triples and keeping them linked to related content items. A comprehensive discussion on triple stores and requirements for their integration in a CMS is presented in [10].

8.3 KRES: Towards for CMS Essential Requirements

The essential requirements identified in the previous section can be successfully implemented in each single CMS platform. Nevertheless, this option leads to adopting design decisions and implementation solutions that hardly can be reused by developers of different CMS platforms. The IKS approach for enabling semantic capabilities in CMS is to develop a software framework providing reusable components for upgrading a CMS to a sCMS. In other words, IKS commits to reusability of semantic components that can be easily integrated in potentially any CMS platform, thus reducing the implementation effort for CMS providers by limiting it to the sole peculiarities of brand new features required by their customers. According to this approach, the IKS project has developed a set of software components that implement the essential semantic web requirements for a sCMS, which are released in the form of RESTful services and Java API. The adoption of RESTful interfaces guarantees the maximum degree of interoperability with existing CMS platforms. KReS, briefly described in this section, is a subset of these components in charge of providing CMS with support for knowledge representation and reasoning capabilities. In order to demonstrate the effectiveness of the IKS software, the scenario described above has been prototyped by the IKS developer team and corresponding demo can be accessed online[5].

KReS consists in three main components: (i) the ontology network manager (ONM), which supports scope-based management of ontologies and interaction with the web of data, (ii) Semion, which supports data reengineering and refactoring to RDF, and (iii) the rule and inference manager, which supports rule definition and automatic reasoning. We briefly describe below the main characteristics of KReS, for additional details the reader can refer to [1].

---

[5] The prototype of the integrity check for external data has been developed by the CNR team and is accessible at http://150.146.88.63:9191/kres/documentation/demo

8.3.1 Ontology Network Manager (ONM)

The Ontology Network Manager (ONM) is responsible for providing ontology network usage, management, and maintenance functionalities. It provides methods for the exploitation of ontology networks, and relies on external persistence storage components (it is integrated with the IKS persistence layer, cf. [11]) for storing the customized scopes and sessions.

ONM provides an implementation for the 4th, 5th, and 6th essential requirements (according to the list presented in Section describing essential requirements). Specific functionalities for supporting reuse and sharing of patterns are part of ONM ongoing development, while it allows managing ontologies, and enables scope-based reasoning on them by defining the concepts of *scope* and *session*. A scope stores ontology networks or parts of them that are to be used for certain purposes. A developer can create a scope and load on it the ontologies that are needed for a certain task. Let us take the integrity check scenario; a developer would load in its associated scope those ontologies against which the integrity check has to be performed. If the same developer needs to use different ontologies for another task e.g. transforming a set of RDF data according to a new ontology, she will create another scope for this task and load on it the target ontologies for the transformation.

Figure 8.5 describes the structure of a scope. In the *Core* space of a scope, read-only ontologies are loaded. Typically they are ontologies that either are external—hence their authoring is owned by third parties, or cannot be changed arbitrarily. Core spaces are shared among all clients using a same KReS instantiation. The *Custom* space of a scope stores all extensions to the ontologies loaded in the Core. Also the Custom space is shared among all clients using a same instantiation of KReS and its content can be changed. Such changes will affect the whole scope environment. As a consequence, possible reasoning operations executed on a scope will be based on both the Core and the Custom space. Finally, a *Session*, is a local environment, typically used for in-memory operations. Sessions allow performing temporary changes to ontologies and executing reasoning operations without affecting the whole scope environment.

Through ONM, it is possible to...

- create, change and delete scopes;
- activate and de-activate scopes;
- add, modify and remove ontologies within a given scope (accessing its custom space);
- create, modify, delete and store session spaces.

8.3.2 Semion

Semion is a set of components addressing the 3rd of our list of essential requirements. It supports:

8 Essential Requirements for Semantic CMS

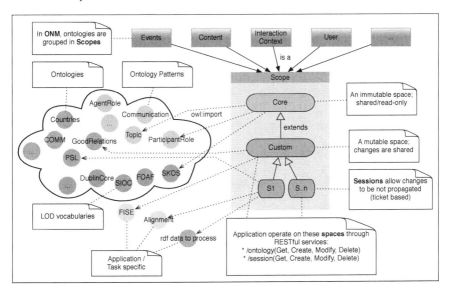

Fig. 8.5: Description of a scope and its parts, as they are realized by the Ontology Network Component.

1. transformation of legacy, non-RDF data sources to RDF;
2. refactoring of RDF datasets by the means of recipes of rules that define alignment and/or refactoring patterns.

Semion approach divides the reengineering process (1) from the modelling one, which is performed through iterations of refactoring actions (2). The reengineering process triplifies the source according to an OWL description of the source data structure. For example, if the data source is a relational database, triplification will be performed according to an OWL model describing a relational database metamodel. The refactoring process is based on the execution of rules defining the criteria for transforming a RDF source to a new one e.g. transforming RDF data based on the DBPedia ontology to data represented by the Google Rich Snippet vocabulary. Semion includes the following components:

- Manager: is the top-level component of Semion. It provides services for starting a reengineering session or a refactoring session, for storing and fetching generated or transformed data sets (via the ONM). It also hides all the details of Semion processes to other services or components interacting with it, and is able to manage several reengineering plugins that implement conversions of different data source types e.g. XML, RDBMS, etc.
- Reengineer(s): are components able to transform specific types of data sources to RDF. KReS alpha supports XML and Relation database source types (iCal and RSS formats are currently under development). The reengineering process performs the transformation from the original data source to RDF without making

semantic assumptions at the domain level. Domain-specific transformations are left to refactoring iterations.
- Refactor: is the responsible of the transformation of RDF datasets to new ones. The refactor allows executing recipes i.e. set of rules to be executed in sequence for a specific transformation, on a RDF dataset e.g. the result of a previous reengineering process. Refactored data sets are stored by using a KReS session in its associated scope.

8.3.3 Rule and Inference Manager (RIM)

Reasoning capabilities are provided by the Rule and Inference Manager (RMI), which addresses the 6th of our list of essential requirements. RMI is responsible for managing rules, and executing reasoning tasks. It supports the management of reasoning patterns, called in this context recipes. Basic functions provided by RMI includes:

- creation, storage, change, and deletion of rules;
- aggregation of rules into recipes that can be stored, and reused for future needs;
- creation, storage, change, and deletion of recipes;
- basic DL reasoning and rule execution.

RMI supports the KReS Rule syntax defined in order to be compatible with SWRL rules as well as SPARQL rules (future work includes support for RIF [5] core syntax). RMI relies on the ONM for managing rules and recipes. It provides a built-in reasoner i.e. Hermit[6], as well as support for pluggin external reasoners through the OWLLink protocol [12].

8.4 Related Work

A number of researches have approached the problem of exploiting semantic technologies for managing content. Sheth et al. [19] describe a software engine that supports the development of semantic-based applications that provide context-sensitive search, browsing, correlation, normalization, and content analysis. Rector and Stevens [17] discuss issues that arise when using OWL in developing knowledge driven applications, with particular focus on a software engineering perspective. Lombardi [13] highlights a number of requirements for better organizing content that facilitate its access with particular focus on enabling easier composition of pages in a CMS.

The advent of the Semantic Web and the recent growing of linking open data caused the emergence of a number of software tools and services that allow to enrich

---

[6] http://hermit-reasoner.com/

content by exploiting natural language techniques integrated with the exploitation of the Linked Data cloud. The OpenCalais platform (http://www.opencalais.com) is a free Natural Language Processing (NLP) system for the delivery of RDF data that identify facts, entities and events extracted from unstructured text. Calais clients have been implemented as modules for Alfresco (http://www.alfresco.com) and Drupal (http://drupal.org). Relation discovery based on NLP and Linked Data is also a key focus of the Zemanta engine (http://www.zemanta.com). Another relation discovery platform based on Semantic Web technologies is the Silk framework [8]. Silk supports the discovery of new links between different RDF data sets.

8.5 Conclusion

With the advent of the Semantic Web and the recent publishing of huge open linked data new opportunities for Content Management System (CMS) have emerged. The Web of Data can serve as a big shared knowledge base for enriching CMS local knowledge and content base. In addition, the formal nature of models underlying linked data i.e. ontologies, allows to exploit semantic technologies for further enrichment and exploitation of the knowledge embedded by a CMS. In this chapter, we have analyzed and discussed, through a sample scenario, the essential requirements that a CMS has to address in order to upgrade to a so-called semantic CMS (sCMS). It came out that such requirements are seven, namely (i) content lifting and enrichment, (ii) exploitation of semantic web resources, (iii) data reengineering and refactoring to semantic web standards, (iv) ontology and rule management, (v) sharing and reuse of ontology patterns, (vi) scope-based reasoning, and (vii) Triple storage. Finally, we have briefly described a set of software services, developed in the context of the Interactive Knowledge Stack project, that address part of such requirements and discussed relevant related work.

Acknowledgments

The work described in this chapter is a teamwork result. The analysis of requirements for the IKS knowledge representation and reasoning layer [2] has been conducted in collaboration with Alessandro Adamou, Eva Blomqvist, Andrea Giovanni Nuzzolese and Aldo Gangemi. The main developers of KReS are Alessandro Adamou, Elvio Concetto Bonafede, Enrico Daga, and Andrea Giovanni Nuzzolese.

References

1. Adamou, A., Blomqvist, E., Bonafede, C., Daga, E., Nuzzolese, A., Presutti, V.: Knowledge Representation and Reasoning System (KReS) – Alpha version report. Tech. rep., IKS Consortium (2010)
2. Adamou, A., Blomqvist, E., Gangemi, A., Nuzzolese, A.G., Presutti, V., Behrendt, W., Damjanovic, V., Conconi, A.: IKS Deliverable 3.2: Ontological Requirements for Industrial CMS Applications. Tech. rep., IKS Consortium (2010)
3. Adida, B., Birbeck, M., McCarron, S., Pemberton, S.: RDFa in XHTML: Syntax and Processing – A Collection of Attributes and Processing Rules for Extending XHTML to Support RDF (2008). URL http://www.w3.org/TR/rdfa-syntax/
4. Bizer, C., Heath, T., Berners-Lee, T.: Linked Data – The Story So Far. International Journal on Semantic Web and Information Systems pp. 1–22 (2009)
5. Boley, H., Hallmark, G., Kifer, M., Brook, S., Paschke, A., Polleres, A., Reynolds, D.: Rif core dialect (2010). URL http://www.w3.org/TR/rif-core/
6. Gangemi, A., Presutti, V.: Ontology design patterns. In: S. Staab, R. Studer (eds.) Handbook on Ontologies, 2 edn., pp. 221–243. Springer, Heidelberg, Germany (2009)
7. Google: Rich snippets (2011). URL http://www.google.com/support/webmasters/bin/answer.py?hl=en&answer=99170
8. Isele, R., Jentzsch, A., Bizer, C.: Silk Server – Adding missing Links while consuming Linked Data. In: Proceedings of the 1st International Workshop on Consuming Linked Data. Shanghai, China (2010)
9. Kasper, W., Steffen, J., Nuzzolese, A.G., Presutti, V.: IKS Deliverable 3.3: Requirements for Semantic Lifting / Wrapping Components. Tech. rep., IKS Consortium (2010)
10. Laleci, G.B., Kilic, O., Aluc, G., Dogac, A., Sinaci, A., Tuncer, F.: IKS Deliverable 3.4: Semantic Data Access and Persistence Requirements Specification. Tech. rep., IKS Consortium (2010)
11. Laleci, G.B., Kilic, O., Cimen, C.: IKS Deliverable 5.4 Intermediate Report – Semantic Data Access and Persistence Components Semantic Data Access and Persistence Components. Tech. rep., IKS Consortium (2010)
12. Liebig, T., Luther, M., Noppens, O., Rodriguez, M., Calvanese, D., Wessel, M., Horridge, M., Bechhofer, S., Tsarkov, D., Sirin, E.: OWLlink: DIG for OWL 2. In: Proceedings of the 5th International Workshop on The OWL: Experiences and Direction (OWLED 2008). Karlsruhe, Germany (2008)
13. Lombardi, V.: Smarter Content Publishing (2002). URL http://www.digital-web.com/articles/smarter_content_publishing/
14. Manola, F., Miller, E.: RDF Primer (2004). URL http://www.w3.org/TR/rdf-primer/
15. Miles, A., Bechhofer, S.: SKOS Simple Knowledge Organization System Reference (2009). URL http://www.w3.org/TR/skos-reference/
16. amd P. F. Patel-Schneider, I.H., Boley, H., Tabet, S., Grosof, B., Dean, M.: SWRL: A Semantic Web Rule Language Combining OWL and RuleML (2004). URL http://www.daml.org/2004/11/fol/rules-all. W3C
17. Rector, A., Stevens, R.: Barriers to the use of OWL in Knowledge Driven Applications. In: Proceedings of the 5th International Workshop on The OWL: Experiences and Direction (OWLED 2008). Karlsruhe, Germany (2008)
18. Romanelli, M., Germesin, S., Adamou, A., Damianovic, V., Janzen, S., Filler, A., Conconi, A., Kowatsch, T., Becker, T.: IKS Deliverable 3.1: Model of Knowledge Based Interaction. Tech. rep., IKS Consortium (2010)
19. Sheth, A., Bertram, C., Avant, D., Hammond, B., Kochut, K., Warke, Y.: Managing semantic content for the web. IEEE Internet Computing 6(4), 80–87 (2002)
20. W3C OWL Working Group: OWL 2 Web Ontology Language Document Overview (2009). URL http://www.w3.org/TR/owl2-overview/
21. W3C SWEO Community Project: Main page (2010). URL http://esw.w3.org/SweoIG/TaskForces/CommunityProjects/LinkingOpenData

Biographical Notes

Valentina Presutti received her Ph.D in Computer Science in 2006 at the University of Bologna (Italy). Currently, she is a researcher at the Semantic Technology Laboratory of the National Research Council (CNR) in Rome. She is one of the key researchers in the EU funded projects NeOn (Networked Ontologies—methods and tool for design of networked ontologies) and IKS (Interactive Knowledge Stack—A framework for Semantic CMS that bring semantics at the interaction level). She has published in international journals / conferences / workshops on topics such as Semantic Web and ontology design. She also teaches Knowledge Management at the University of Bologna. Her research interests include Semantic Web, ontology design, knowledge patterns, linked data analysis and consumption, collaborative knowledge/content management, and ontology-based software engineering.

Part III
Evaluation and Profiles of 27 CMS Provider Companies

Chapter 9
Evaluation of Content Management Systems

Tobias Kowatsch and Wolfgang Maass

Abstract In this part of the book we provide results from an online survey targeting companies of Content Management Systems (CMSs). The objective of this survey is to provide an overview of the capabilities of today's CMSs, in particular with regard to the adoption of semantic technologies. The survey has been promoted as part of the European Project Interactive Knowledge Stack (IKS, iks-project.eu). It was available online from June to November 2010. Overall, 27 CMS companies have been selected for publication in the current book. Accordingly, detailed profiles are available for each CMS provider company. These profiles are now available for IT executives of potential CMS customers to make decisions on which CMS providers fit best to their business. This chapter provides an overview of the survey methodology and descriptive statistics before each profile is presented.

9.1 Introduction

Content Management Systems (CMSs) are used in almost every industry by millions of end-user organizations around the world. In contrast to the 90s, they are no longer used as isolated applications in one organization today but they support business critical core operations in business ecosystems, for instance, in the media sector for eCommerce transactions. In addition, applications such as Facebook, Youtube, Google Maps, Twitter or Scribd show that content management today is more interactive and more integrative: interactive because end-users are increasingly content

---

Tobias Kowatsch
Research Associate, Institute of Technology Management, University of St. Gallen, Switzerland, e-mail: `tobias.kowatsch@unisg.ch`

Wolfgang Maass
Chair in Information and Service Systems (ISS), Faculty of Law and Economics, Saarland University, Germany, e-mail: `wolfgang.maass@iss.uni-saarland.de`

creators themselves and integrative because content elements can be embedded into various other applications as well.

The EU project IKS investigates how Semantic Technologies (e.g., RDF, Microformats, OWL, SPARQL, SWRL among many others) can increase interactivity and integration capabilities of CMSs and how they provide business value to millions of CMS end-user organisations with semantically enriched data (e.g., from DBPedia, CIA Factbook, UK census data etc.).

As part of the IKS project, the Institute of Technology Management at University of St. Gallen together with Salzburg Research and the Germany Research Center for Artificial Intelligence have conducted an online survey in 2010 that targeted provider firms of CMSs. The objective of this survey is to provide an overview of today's CMS capabilities including the use of Semantic Technologies that are relevant to IT executives of potential CMS customers. In this sense, IT executives can use this information to select relevant CMS provider companies that best fit their business. The contribution of this chapter is threefold: First, we provide details on the survey methodology in the next Section. Then, the results are presented in the form of descriptive statistics and by the profiles of 27 CMS provider companies.

9.2 Methodology

The design of the survey and its items have been adapted from prior research [1, 2]. The survey instrument is presented in Table 9.1.

Table 9.1: Survey instrument

Category	Survey item / instructions
Management Summary	Interactive Knowledge Stack (IKS) is an Integrating Project part-funded by the European Commission. It will provide an open source technology platform for semantically enhanced content management systems (CMSs) by 2012. The objective of this survey is to evaluate CMSs for a book that will be relevant to IT executives of potential CMS customers. This survey targets therefore CMS provider firms that want to be visible in that book by providing information of their CMSs. The book will be published in the first quarter of 2011. The survey will take you approx. 25 minutes to complete. Please take your time as your input will be verified by our partners from Salzburg Research and the German Research Center for Artificial Intelligence. With your agreement, we will create a link to the website of your company on the IKS portal after you have completed this survey. All information provided by you will be only used within our project and for the book publication process. Personal information is important and required to verify your inputs.
Personal Details	Name, e-Mail address, phone number, job position

9 Evaluation of Content Management Systems

Survey instrument (continued)

Category	Survey item / instructions

Company overview	- Name, website and contact details
	- Number of employees?
	- Name, version and release date of the CMS?
	- Short description of the CMS
	- In which countries do you have a branch office?
	- Where is your main market in terms of customer size?
	    – Micro enterprises with less than 10 employees
	    – Small enterprises with less than 50 employees
	    – Medium enterprises with less than 250 employees
	    – Large enterprises with more than 250 employees
	- Do you focus on a particular industry or sector (vertical market) with your CMS or is it targeted at a variety of businesses (horizontal market)?
	    – Horizontal / Vertical / for which industry
	- What are your top three reference customers?

CMS overview	- When was the first version of your CMS provided to a customer? (Year)
	- Which documentation is available for your CMS? (Web-based documentation / printed handbook)
	    – Documentation for Authors/ Editors
	    – Documentation for Administrators
	    – Documentation for Developers
	- In which languages is the CMS available?
	- Which technical skills are required to use the CMS?
	    – Technical skills required by the administrator
	    – Technical skills required by the content author
	- How long does it usually take a customer to learn the CMS (in days)?
	    – How long does it take the administrator
	    – How long does it take the content author

License Model	- Are potential customers able to run and test the CMS before signing a contract? – yes – link to the trial version / no - Pricing for workstation license (approx. in EUR, further information) - Pricing for server license (approx. in EUR, further information) - Pricing for ASP / Cloud license (approx. in EUR, further information) - No licence fee at all / open source model

Survey instrument (continued)

Category	Survey item / instructions
Service and Support	Which kind of service and support do you offer to your customers? • E-Mail support • Phone support • Remote support • On-site support • Others / More details • Pricing for service and support licence
Technologies that are used along the CMS stack	• Operating Systems: Microsoft Windows, Linux, Unix, Apple OS X, Others / More details • Database Management Systems: Microsoft SQL Server, IBM DB2, Oracle Database, Oracle MySQL, PostgreSQL, Apache CouchDB, Others / More details • Data Formats: Database fields, XML, RDF, RDFa, Others / More details • Metadata Models: NewsML, Dublin Core (DC), Friend of a Friend (FOAF), Semantically-Interlinked Online Communities (SIOC), Exchangeable Image File Format (EXIF), Simple Knowledge Organisation System (SKOS), GoodRelations Product Ontology, Smart Product Description Object (SPDO), Others / More details • Microformats: hCard, hCalendar, hReview, VoteLinks, Others • Database or knowledge representation languages: SQL, JCR Version 1 (JSR 170), OWL, RDF Schema, Others / More details • Supported Query Languages for Content: SQL, SPARQL, XPath, XQuery, Others / More details • Supported Indexing Mechanisms: Lucene, SOLr, Others / More details • Supported Rule Languages / Reasoning Languages: SWRL, RIF, Others / More details • Supported Business Process Languages: BPML, BPEL, jBPM, Drools, Others / More details • Implementation Languages: HTML, CSS, PHP, ASP, Java, Ruby, Python, .NET, C, C#, C++, Others / More details • Supported Presentation Formats and Mechanisms: HTML 4, HTML 5, XHTML, Flash, PDF, CSS, RSS, Text-to-audio, XSLT, Others / More details

Survey instrument (continued)

Category	Survey item / instructions
Features of the CMS	• Supported Generic Interfaces: 　– CMIS 1.0 　– JCR (JSR 170) 　– Others / More details • Supported Interfaces to existing platforms: 　– Integration of YouTube content 　– Integration of Twitter content 　– Integration of Facebook content 　– Notifications to Twitter 　– Notifications to Facebook 　– Others / More details • Support for Content Creation: 　– Provides related links during content creation to the author 　– Provides related documents during content creation to the author 　– Provides related video clips during content creation to the author 　– Others / More details
Features of the CMS	• Supported Workflows: 　– Supports fundamental process primitives (e.g., forking, merging, choice points) for the specification of workflows by the CMS customer 　– Supports a publication workflow with at least two CMS authors involved 　– Event-based triggering of emails Event-based triggering of SMS messages 　– Event-based triggering of MMS messages 　– Event-based triggering of FAX messages 　– Event-based triggering of messages to Twitter 　– Event-based triggering of messages to Facebook 　– Others / More details • Supported Devices to Access Content: 　– HTML client on Desktop PC 　– HTML client on Mobile Device 　– Native desktop application 　– Native mobile application 　– Others / More details

Survey instrument (continued)

Category	Survey item / instructions
Features of the CMS	• Supported devices to create content: – HTML client on desktop PC – HTML client on mobile device – Native desktop application – Native mobile application – Others / More details • Supported personalization features: – Personalized content author interface – Personalized end-user / consumer interface – Creation of personalized newsletters – Others / More details • Support for automated content enrichment: – Semi-automated creation of links for named entities (e.g., recognition of a city and creation of a Link to Wikipedia) – Automated creation of links for named entities – Semi-automated creation of tags to content (e.g. suggestion-based) – Automated creation of tags to content – Others / More details • Supported features for an intuitive user interface: – Drag 'n Drop for structuring menu items – Drag 'n Drop for placing content items on a page layout – Drag 'n Drop for uploading documents to the CMS – WYSIWYG-Editor for content authors – Undo / Redo – Others / More details • Support for enhanced content search: – Faceted search (filtering of search results by categories) – Search term suggestions when typing the query – Formal query language support – Others / More details

9 Evaluation of Content Management Systems 117

Survey instrument (continued)

Category	Survey item / instructions

Features of the CMS	• Support for content modelling:
	  – Creation of a content type with a particular structure (e.g., for defining forms to be filled by end users, or presentation templates for specific kinds of information)
	  – Others / More details
	• Supported CMS performance features:
	  – Load Balancing
	  – Page Caching
	  – Static Content Export
	  – Database Replication
	  – Others / More details
	• On which levels are access restrictions implemented?
	  – Archive-level
	  – Project-level
	  – Folder-level
	  – Document-level
	  – Part-of-document-level
	  – Group-level (role-level)
	  – Others / More details

The survey was online from June to November 2010 and it took approximately 25 minutes for each CMS provider to complete it. Personal information was required to get in contact with the CMS provider if any information provided was unclear. On request, a copy of the data was sent to the e-mail address of the CMS provider. Furthermore, each participant had to confirm explicitly that the information provided is going to be published in the current book.

In order to ask CMS provider companies to participate in the survey, Salzburg Research has promoted the survey by several promotion activities (see Table 9.2 for further details). Then, after the deadline of the survey, a in-depth review process was conducted by Salzburg Research, the German Center for Artificial Intelligence and the Institute of Technology Management at University of St. Gallen (ITEM-HSG). Accordingly, quality assurance guidelines have been developed as shown in Table 9.3. Based on these guidelines, decisions have been made to accept, revise or drop entries of the CMS providers. In case a revision of an entry was required, e.g., if some of the information provided was unclear, the CMS provider was asked to provide the corresponding information. Overall, the review process took two months.

Table 9.2: Survey promotion conducted by Salzburg Research

No	Target outlet / community	URL
CMS Survey Announcements		
1	IKS project website	http://iks-project.eu/iks-survey-book-semantic-capabilities-content-management-systems

Survey promotion conducted by Salzburg Research (continued)

No	Target outlet / community	URL
2	JSFCentral	http://www.jsfcentral.com/
3	CMSWire	http://www.cmswire.com/cms/web-cms/be-a-pal-help-iks-bring-semantic-technologies-to-cms-008057.php
4	CMSMatrix	http://www.cmsmatrix.org/matrix/news/iks-invites-cms-vendors-to-online-survey-about-semantic-technologies2
5	CMS Forum	http://www.cms-forum.org/
6	GigaOM	http://gigaom.com/
7	Techweb	http://www.techweb.com/
8	The Content Wrangler	http://thecontentwrangler.com/
9	Content Here	http://www.contenthere.net/
10	Contentinople	http://www.contentinople.com/
11	Friendfeed	http://friendfeed.com/cococomm/eb47255f/be-pal-help-iks-bring-semantic-technologies-to
12	Michelle Manafy Twitter stream (EContentMag.com)	http://twitter.com/michellemanafy
13	Drupal website	http://drupal.org/node/849446
14	Semanticweb.com	http://www.semanticweb.com/news/cms_vendors_have_opportunity_to_get_semantic_168606.asp
15	ReadWriteWeb	http://readwriteweb.com/
16	SemWiki.org	http://www.semwiki.org/
17	The Semantic Web Gang	http://semanticgang.talis.com/
18	Fresh Knowledge	http://www.freshknowledge.net/
19	Wikimedia	http://wikimedia.org/
20	Semantic Web Coordination Group	http://www.w3.org/2001/sw/CG/
21	Digg	http://digg.com/tech_news/IKS_Invites_CMS_Vendors_to_Online_Survey_about_Semantic_Tech
22	PHPLens	http://phplens.com/
23	Slashdot	http://slashdot.org/
24	OSnews	http://www.osnews.com/
25	PHPDeveloper	http://www.phpdeveloper.org/
26	The Server Side	http://www.theserverside.com/
27	DownloadSquad	http://downloadsquad.switched.com/
28	PHPBuilder	http://www.phpbuilder.com/
29	Ngoid	http://ngoid.sourceforge.net/
30	Blog of Henri Bergius	http://bergie.iki.fi/blog/
31	InfoToday	http://www.infotoday.com/
32	CMSCritic	http://www.cmscritic.com/
33	Semanticbot1	http://semanticbot1.blogspot.com
34	IXThemes	http://ixthemes.org/modules/wp/?p=2557
35	OpenSource-news	http://www.opensource-news.com/cms/drupal/iks-invites-cms-vendors-to-online-survey-about-semantic-technologies
36	Knowledge Solutions	http://knowledge-solutions.com/aggregator

9 Evaluation of Content Management Systems

Survey promotion conducted by Salzburg Research (continued)

No	Target outlet / community	URL
37	Commerce Companion	http://www.thecommercecompanion.com/aggregator/categories/3
38	Frenzy Blogging	http://www.frenzyblogging.com/2010/07/16/be-a-pal-help-iks-bring-semantic-technologies-to-cms/
39	Content Management System Software	http://www.contentmanagementsystemsoftware.info/more/IKS-Invites-CMS-Vendors-to-Online-Survey-about-16.Semantic-?l=aHR0cDovL2RydXBhbC5vcmcvbm9kZS84NDk0NDY=&k=
40	Interactive Online	https://interactiveonline.com/drupal/iks-invites-cms-vendors-to-online-survey-about-semantic-technologies
41	Java Dzone	http://java.dzone.com/
E-Mail invitations		
1	IKS CMS Community – (approx. 80 CMS Vendors aware of IKS)	
2	IKS Community Mailing list	
3	IKS Industry partners	
4	CMS Vendor community; approx. 350 CMS Vendors – includes list from Contentmanager.de, first contact with IKS	
5	Open Source CMS Providers: approx. 188 OS projects, first contact with IKS	

Table 9.3: Quality assurance guidelines for the entries of the survey

No	Guideline
1	Any typos must be corrected.
2	Any entries from non-CMS providers (e.g., CMS plug-in providers) must be dropped
3	Feedback must be consolidated if a CMS provider has participated twice in the survey (the most recent entry should be used as basis, cross-check with the contact person, if something is unclear)
4	All personal details should have been provided (e.g., name, email, phone and job position)
5	All company details should have been provided (from name, website, address to the three reference customers)
6	All CMS details should have been provided (from the year of the first release to the technical skills of a customer)
7	All License details should have been provided. Exception: Further Information is optional. Note: license fees could be provided in form of a price range
8	All service and support details should have been provided. Note: service and support fees may have a price range
9	The following categories of the technology stack should have been provided: Operating System, DBMS, Data Formats, database / knowledge representation language, query language for content, implementation language, presentation format / mechanism
10	The last section on 'CMS features' is optional

No	Guideline
11	If the CMS provider does not want his data to be published in the book, the contact person must be asked if he or she is confident with that decision
12	If there is relevant information missing, reviewers should use the provider's web site to clarify the issue and ask the contact person in order to get the corresponding information

9.3 Results

In summary, 225 entries have been analysed from which 27 profiles of CMSs have been selected for publication in the current book. The most entries have been dropped because of missing data, duplicate entries or entries that were not related to CMS provider companies. The CMS providers participated from thirteen countries as shown in Fig. 9.1. Almost all of them are micro enterprises to large enterprises (cf. Fig. 9.2) with rather mature CMS products, i.e. the first release was before 2006 (cf. Fig. 9.3). The CMS provider companies serve mostly medium and large customer organizations (cf. Fig. 9.4).

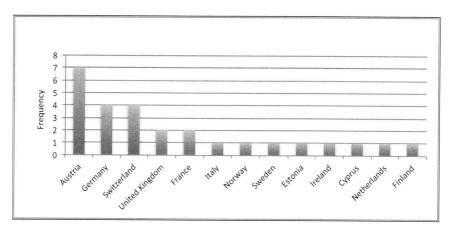

Fig. 9.1: Distribution of CMS provider companies by country

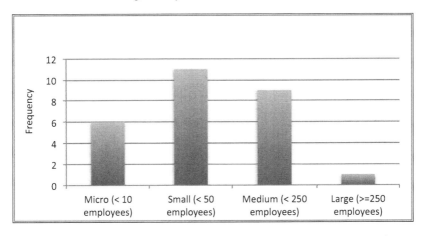

Fig. 9.2: Distribution of the CMS provider companies by employee size

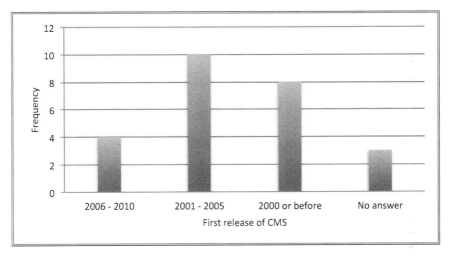

Fig. 9.3: Distribution of the first release of the CMS provider company's products indicating the maturity of the CMSs

9.4 Profiles of CMS Provider Companies

In this section, the profiles of 27 CMS provider companies are listed alphabetically. They have been assigned to two categories. First, 21 profiles of CMS providers are listed that provide CMSs with no specific industry focus, i.e. horizontal CMSs. Second, six profiles are listed with a specific industry focus, i.e. vertical CMSs (e.g., CMS for tourism or the media industry).

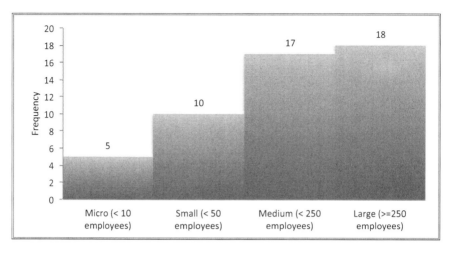

Fig. 9.4: Distribution of enterprises (i.e. CMS customers) targeted by the CMS provider companies. Note: multiple answers were allowed

9.4.1 CMS with No Specific Industry Focus

An overview of these CMS provider companies is listed below. The name of the CMS is provided in brackets.

1. Alfresco, United Kingdom (Alfresco)
2. Alkacon Software GmbH, Germany (OpenCMS)
3. Brunner AG, Switzerland (mirusys)
4. Day Software AG (now part of Adobe), Switzerland (CQ5)
5. Dynamic Works, Cyprus (EasyConsole CMS)
6. EPiServer AB, Sweden (EPiServer CMS)
7. Gentics Software GmbH, Austria (Gentics Content.Node)
8. GOSS Interactive Ltd, United Kingdom (GOSS iCM)
9. Homepage Toolbox, Austria (Homepage Toolbox)
10. Jahia Solutions Group, Switzerland (Jahia)
11. Jarn AS, Norway (Plone)
12. Klein & Partner KG, BlueDynamics Alliance, Austria (Plone)
13. Magnolia International Ltd., Switzerland (Magnolia CMS)
14. MASSIVE ART WebServices GmbH, Austria (ZOOLU)
15. Nemein Oy, Finland (Midgard)
16. Modera, Estonia (Modera Webmaster)
17. NexxaCon IT-Consulting GmbH, Austria (join2learn)
18. Nuxeo, France (NUXEO)
19. Ooffee, France (Apache Lenya)
20. punkt. netServices GmbH, Austria (conX)
21. semsol, Germany (Paggr CMS)

9.4.2 CMS with a Specific Industry Focus

An overview of the CMS provider companies is listed below. The name of the CMS and industry focus are provided in brackets.

1. CIC Creative Internet Consulting GmbH, Germany (packagemaster: tourism industry)
2. Hippo B.V., The Netherlands (Hippo CMS: government, publishing and medical industries)
3. PAUX Technologies GmbH, Germany (PAUX: publishing houses and content providers)
4. QuinScape GmbH, Germany (OpenSAGA: government)
5. TERMINALFOUR, Ireland (TERMINALFOUR Site Manager: Higher Education, Government, Retail & Finance)
6. TXT Polymedia, Italy (TXT Polymedia: Newspapers, TV Broadcasters, Telcos)

References

1. Kowatsch, T., Maass, W., Damjanovic, V., Behrendt, W., Gruber, A., Nagel, B., Sauer, S., Engels, G.: IKS Deliverable - D1.1 Report: Design of the Semantic Benchmark Experiment. Tech. rep., IKS Consortium (2009)
2. Stahl, F., Maass, W.: Content Management Handbuch: Strategien, Theorien und Systeme für erfolgreiches Content Management. NetAcademy Press, St. Gallen, Switzerland (2003)

Biographical Notes

Tobias Kowatsch is research associate at the Institute of Technology Management, University of St. Gallen. His research interests in the management of information systems are the adoption and diffusion of innovations, consumer behaviour, mobile business, smart products, internet of things and recommendation agents. He studied Computer Science in Media at Hochschule Furtwangen University (HFU) in Germany and wrote his Diploma thesis about semantic web applications in 2005. After studying in Scotland and doing social volunteering in South Africa, he attended the Master's programme in Computer Science in Media at HFU in 2006 and passed with distinction. Then, he did empirical research on the user acceptance of mobile information systems at the Research Center for Intelligent Media at HFU.

Wolfgang Maass holds a Chair in Information and Service Systems (ISS) at the faculty of Law and Economics of the Saarland University, Germany. Prior to that, he has led the Smart Products research group at the Institute of Technology Management (ITEM) at the University of St. Gallen, Switzerland and the Research Center for Intelligent Media (RCIM) at Furtwangen University, Germany. In 1996, he completed his Ph.D. in Computer Science at Saarland University. He was awarded with a habilitation in Business Administration with special focus on Information Management by the Department of Management at University of St. Gallen in 2007.

His research focuses on understanding design methodologies for complex Information Systems and in particular Ubiquitous Information Systems and Intelligent Information Systems. Emphasis is given to the analysis of full product design cycles, including creating and empirical evaluation of innovative Information Systems. His current interest is on the design of situated Information Systems by leveraging semantic technologies, multi-modal communication technologies, and technologies from the Internet of Things (IOT) and Internet of Services (IOS).

He is a member of the editorial board of Electronic Markets and a reviewer for the European Journal of Information Systems, Decision Support Systems, the International Journal on Media Management, and the Journal of Theoretical and Applied Electronic Commerce Research.

Chapter 10
CMS with No Particular Industry Focus

10.1 Alfresco, United Kingdom: Alfresco

Management Summary

Web, e-Mail	www.alfresco.com, info@alfresco.com
Address	The Place, Bridge Street, Maidenhead, SL6 1AF, UK
CMS release	Alfresco 3.3 (May 2010)
Number of employees	approx. 135
Branch offices	UK, USA, France, Germany, Australia
Targeted customers	Small to large enterprises
Reference customers	http://www.alfresco.com/customers/
First version of CMS	2005
Short description of the CMS	Alfresco is the leading open source enterprise content management system built by the most experienced team in the industry drawn from Documentum®, Vignette® and Interwoven®. Product features include Document Management, Records Management and Web Content Management. France, Germany, Australia
Licensing	No licence fee at all; Trial: http://wiki.alfresco.com/wiki/Download_Community_Edition

Overview of the CMS

Documentation of CMS	Web-based documentation for Authors/Editors, Web-based documentation and printed handbook for Administrators and Developers
Supported languages of the CMS	English, French, German, Italian, Japanese, Spanish
Technical skills required for CMS use	Administrator: Depends on scale of installation: for a small installation with no customizations, basic operating system and database knowledge are needed, primarily for backup management; for larger installations, Java, Java Application Server, OS and RDBMS administration skills are beneficial. Supported stacks: http://www.alfresco.com/services/subscription/supported-platforms/3-x/ Content author: Use of browser
Time to learn to use the CMS	Administrator: 2 – 5 days; Content author: 1 – 2 days
Service and support	E-Mail support, Phone support, Remote support, On-site support

SUPPORTED TECHNOLOGIES

Operating systems	Microsoft Windows, Linux, Unix, Apple OS X
Database management systems	Microsoft SQL Server, IBM DB2, Oracle Database, Oracle MySQL, PostgreSQL
Data formats	Dublin Core (DC), Exchangeable Image File Format (EXIF), Fully customizable
Metadata models	XML
Microformats	n/a
Database or knowledge representation languages	JCR Version 1 (JSR 170), CMIS
Query languages for content	XPath, CMISQL
Indexing mechanisms	Lucene
Rule / reasoning languages	n/a
Business process languages	jBPM
Implementation languages	HTML, CSS, Java
Presentation formats and mechanisms	HTML 4 and 5, XHTML, Flash, PDF, CSS, RSS, XSLT

CMS FEATURES

Generic Interfaces	CMIS 1.0, JCR (JSR 170)
Interfaces to existing platforms	WordPress
Support for content creation	n/a
Supported workflows	Supports fundamental process primitives (e.g., forking, merging, choice points) for the specification of workflows by the CMS customer, Supports a publication workflow with at least two CMS authors involved, Event-based triggering of emails
Devices to access content	HTML client on desktop PC and mobile device
Devices to create content	HTML client on desktop PC and mobile device
Personalization features	n/a
Content enrichment	n/a
User interface	WYSIWYG-Editor for content authors
Content search	n/a
Content modelling	Creation of a content type with a particular structure (e.g., for defining forms to be filled by end users, or defining presentation templates for specific kinds of information)
Performance features	Load Balancing, Static Content Export, Database Replication
Access restrictions	Document-level, Group-level (role-level)

10.2 Alkacon Software GmbH, Germany: OpenCms

MANAGEMENT SUMMARY

Web, e-Mail	www.alkacon.com, info@alkacon.com
Address	An der Wachsfabrik 13, 50996 Köln, Germany
CMS release	OpenCms 7.5 (January 2010)
Number of employees	approx. 10
Branch offices	Germany
Targeted customers	Large enterprises
Reference customers	Bayer Business Services CME – Chicago Mercantile Exchange SWITCH
First version of CMS	2000
Short description of the CMS	OpenCms from Alkacon Software is a professional, easy to use website content management system. OpenCms helps content managers worldwide to create and maintain beautiful websites fast and efficiently. The fully browser based user interface features con-figurable editors for structured content with well-defined fields. Alternatively, content can be created using an integrated WYSIWYG editor similar to well known office applications. A sophisticated template engine enforces a site-wide corporate layout and W3C standard compliance for all content. OpenCms is based on Java and XML technology. It can be deployed in an open source environment (e.g. Linux, Apache, Tomcat, MySQL) as well as on commercial components (e.g., Windows NT, IIS, BEA Weblogic, Oracle).
Licensing	Pricing for workstation license: Open Source / LGPL Pricing for server license: Open Source / LGPL Pricing for ASP / Cloud license: Open Source / LGPL No licence fee at all / open source model Trial: http: //wiki.alfresco.com/wiki/Download_Community_Edition

Overview of the CMS

Documentation of CMS	Web-based documentation for authors/editors, administrators and developers
Supported languages of the CMS	English, German, Spanish
Technical skills required for CMS use	Administrator: Installing a Java Servlet Engine (e.g. Tomcat), installing a DB (e.g. mySQL) usually in-stalling Webserver (e.g. Apache httpd). Content author: Office Products like OpenOffice or MS Office
Time to learn to use the CMS	Administrator: 2 days Content author: 2 days
Service and support	E-Mail support, Phone support, Remote support, On-site support, see `http://www.alkacon.com/support`, Pricing: starting at 1 500 Euro

Supported Technologies

Operating systems	Microsoft Windows, Linux, Unix, Apple OS X, Everything where a Java VM can run
Database management systems	Microsoft SQL Server, IBM DB2, Oracle Database, Oracle MySQL, PostgreSQL
Data formats	Database fields, XML
Metadata models	n/a
Microformats	n/a
Database or knowledge representation languages	SQL
Query languages for content	SQL, Java API
Indexing mechanisms	Apache Lucene
Rule / reasoning languages	n/a
Business process languages	n/a
Implementation languages	HTML, CSS, Java
Presentation formats and mechanisms	HTML 4, HTML 5, XHTML, Flash, PDF, CSS, RSS, XSLT

CMS Features

Generic Interfaces	n/a
Interfaces to existing platforms	n/a
Support for content creation	n/a
Supported workflows	Supports a publication workflow with at least two CMS authors involved
Devices to access content	HTML client on desktop PC and mobile device
Devices to create content	HTML client on desktop PC and mobile device
Personalization features	Personalized content author interface, Personalized end-user / consumer interface, Creation of personalized newsletters
Content enrichment	n/a
User interface	Drag 'n Drop for uploading documents to the CMS, WYSIWYG-Editor for content authors, Undo
Content search	n/a
Content modelling	Creation of a content type with a particular structure (e.g., for defining forms to be filled by end users, or defining presentation templates for specific kinds of information)
Performance features	Load Balancing, Page Caching, Static Content Export, Database Replication, Some features like Load Balancing or Database Replication require a commercial extension from Alkacon (Alkacon OCEE)
Access restrictions	Document-level, Group-level (role-level)

10.3 Brunner AG, Druck und Medien, Switzerland: mirusys®

MANAGEMENT SUMMARY

Web, e-Mail	www.bag.ch, info@bag.ch
Address	Arsenalstr. 24, CH-6011 Kriens, Switzerland
CMS release	mirusys 4.1 (2010)
Number of employees	approx. 70
Branch offices	Switzerland
Targeted customers	Micro, small and medium enterprises
Reference customers	n/a
First version of CMS	n/a
Short description of the CMS	The mirusys® Content Management System by Brunner Digital provides the best tools to run your own website. Would you like to maintain your website on your own? Then you keep your website at any time under control with mirusys®, the CMS solution by Brunner AG Druck und Medien. Content updates are just made with one click. But you can also change efficiently the existing structure of your website without any programming skills. You will learn to use this CMS easily due to the intuitive graphical user interface. Web: http://cms.mirusys.ch
Licensing	n/a

OVERVIEW OF THE CMS

Documentation of CMS	Web-based documentation for authors/editors and administrators
Supported languages of the CMS	English, French, German
Technical skills required for CMS use	Content author: online basics
Time to learn to use the CMS	Administrator: 2 days, Content author: 1 day
Service and support	E-Mail support, Phone support, Remote support

Supported Technologies

Operating systems	Linux
Database management systems	Oracle, MySQL
Data formats	XML
Metadata models	n/a
Microformats	n/a
Database or knowledge representation languages	n/a
Query languages for content	XPath
Indexing mechanisms	n/a
Rule / reasoning languages	n/a
Business process languages	n/a
Implementation languages	HTML, CSS, PHP
Presentation formats and mechanisms	HTML 4, XHTML, Flash, PDF, CSS, XSLT

CMS Features

Generic Interfaces	n/a
Interfaces to existing platforms	YouTube and Twitter content
Support for content creation	n/a
Supported workflows	n/a
Devices to access content	n/a
Devices to create content	n/a
Personalization features	n/a
Content enrichment	n/a
User interface	WYSIWYG-Editor for content authors
Content search	n/a
Content modelling	n/a
Performance features	Load Balancing
Access restrictions	n/a

10.4 Day Software (now part of Adobe), Switzerland: CQ5

MANAGEMENT SUMMARY

Web, e-Mail	www.day.com, information@day.com
Address	http://www.day.com/day/en/company/contact_us.html
CMS release	CQ5 (February 2011)
Number of employees	approx. 150
Branch offices	Worldwide, see http://adobe.com/
Targeted customers	Large enterprises
Reference customers	http://www.day.com/day/en/customers.html
First version of CMS	1995
Short description of the CMS	CQ5 Web Content Management, Digital Asset Man-agement, and Social Collaboration form a platform for Web 2.0 that enables interactive marketers to leverage the online channel as the most cost-effective marketing vehicle to engage customers and prospects to increase competitive advantage and drive revenue. Coupled with Day's world-class user experience to unleash marketing's creativity with a fun-to-use, drag-and-drop interface, CQ5 enables marketing to meet key growth challenges.
Licensing	Pricing for server license: Pricing info upon request Trial version available, but no direct download

Overview of the CMS

Documentation of CMS	Web-based documentation for authors/editors, administrators and developers
Supported languages of the CMS	Chinese, English, French, German, Italian, Japanese, Spanish; Note: Any additional language can be configured, the above list is the ones for which we provide translations of the administrative and content creation interfaces out of the box
Technical skills required for CMS use	Administrator: None Content author: None
Time to learn to use the CMS	Administrator: 1 day Content author: 1 day
Service and support	E-Mail support, Phone support, Remote support, On-site support

Supported Technologies

Operating systems	Microsoft Windows, Linux, Unix
Database management systems	Microsoft SQL Server, IBM DB2, Oracle Database, Oracle MySQL, PostgreSQL
Data formats	System can be adapted to various data formats if needed
Metadata models	Dublin Core, system is modular to adapt to various other data formats if needed
Microformats	System can be adapted to various microformats if needed
Database or knowledge representation languages	System can be adapted to various representation languages
Query languages for content	SQL, XPath
Indexing mechanisms	Apache Lucene, Apache SOLr, external indexing systems supported via customizable bridging components
Rule / reasoning languages	n/a
Business process languages	System can be adapted to various business process languages if needed
Implementation languages	Java-based but supports many scripting languages
Presentation formats and mechanisms	Presentation formats can be customized as desired

CMS Features

Generic Interfaces	CMIS 1.0, JCR (JSR 170)
Interfaces to existing platforms	YouTube and Twitter content
Support for content creation	YouTube content, Twitter content, Facebook content, Notifications to Twitter and Facebook
Supported workflows	Provides related links, documents and video clips during content creation to the author; Note: related items are not currently deduced automatically
Devices to access content	Supports fundamental process primitives (e.g., forking, merging, choice points) for the specification of workflows by the CMS customer, supports publication workflow with at least two CMS authors involved; Event-based triggering of emails, SMS messages, MMS messages and FAX messages; Event-based triggering of messages to Twitter and Facebook
Devices to create content	HTML client on desktop PC and mobile device, Note: Native applications can be developed if needed
Personalization features	HTML client on desktop PC and mobile device
Content enrichment	n/a
User interface	Drag 'n Drop for placing content items on a page layout, Drag 'n Drop for uploading documents to the CMS, WYSIWYG-Editor for content authors, Undo, Redo
Content search	Facetted search (filtering of search results by categories), Search term suggestions when typing the query, Query builder tools make search languages unnecessary in many cases
Content modelling	Creation of a content type with a particular structure (e.g., for defining forms to be filled by end users, or defining presentation templates for specific kinds of information), Whole spectrum from fully unstructured to fully structured content modelling is supported
Performance features	Load Balancing, Page Caching, Static Content Export, Database Replication
Access restrictions	Node level, which can be any of the following: ar-chive-level, project-level, folder-level, document-level, part-of-document-level, group-level

10.5 Dynamic Works, Cyprus: EasyConsole CMS

MANAGEMENT SUMMARY

Web, e-Mail	www.dynamicworks.eu, info@dynamicworks.eu
Address	1, Diogenous St. - Block A - 5th Floor - Engomi 2404 Nicosia Cyprus
CMS release	EasyConsole CMS 3.1 (2010)
Number of employees	approx. 15
Branch offices	Cyprus, UK
Targeted customers	Micro enterprises, Small enterprises, Medium enter-prises, Large enterprises
Reference customers	Allgeier DMS Computer, Belgium, Austria Bank of Cyprus UK European University Cyprus
First version of CMS	2003
Short description of the CMS	Your web developer's life has never been easier. EasyConsole CMS provides the technology for developing high-end dynamic websites for your specific vertical market in no time. After the website has been developed it's the end-customer's turn to enjoy the benefits. Fast content updating, live online chat capabilities, powerful administration and external database integration capabilities, content syndication, e-mail and SMS messaging communication alerts, and serious web presence with minimal ongoing operating costs. Important innovation: Seamless integration with EasyConsole CRM
Licensing	Pricing for workstation license: 1 890 EUR (License per URL); Pricing for server license: on request (License for unlimited URLs that belong to the same group) Trial: http://ecv3demo.dwlocal.com/console

Overview of the CMS

Documentation of CMS	Web-based documentation for authors/editors, administrators and developers
Supported languages of the CMS	English, Russian, Greek
Technical skills required for CMS use	Administrator: Talent in web development Content author: Computing skills
Time to learn to use the CMS	Administrator: 2 days Content author: 1 day
Service and support	E-Mail support, Phone support, Remote support, On-site support, HelpDesk – Ticketing System in place, Pricing: 14% on initial fee

Supported Technologies

Operating systems	Microsoft Windows, Linux
Database management systems	Microsoft SQL Server, Oracle Database
Data formats	Database fields, XML, Web Services
Metadata models	NewsML, Dublin Core (DC)
Microformats	n/a
Database or knowledge representation languages	SQL
Query languages for content	SQL
Indexing mechanisms	n/a
Rule / reasoning languages	n/a
Business process languages	n/a
Implementation languages	HTML, CSS, Coldfusion
Presentation formats and mechanisms	HTML 4, HTML 5, XHTML, Flash, PDF, CSS, RSS

CMS Features

Generic Interfaces	n/a
Interfaces to existing platforms	YouTube content, Twitter content, Facebook content, Notifications to Twitter, Notifications to Facebook
Support for content creation	n/a
Supported workflows	Supports fundamental process primitives (e.g., forking, merging, choice points) for the specification of workflows by the CMS customer, Supports a publication workflow with at least two CMS authors involved, Event-based triggering of emails, SMS messages, FAX messages and messages to Twitter and Facebook
Devices to access content	HTML client on desktop PC
Devices to create content	HTML client on desktop PC and on mobile device, Native desktop application, Native mobile application
Personalization features	Personalized content author interface, Personalized end-user / consumer interface, Creation of personalized newsletters
Content enrichment	Semi-automated creation of links for named entities (e.g., recognition of a city and creation of a Link to Wikipedia), Semi-automated creation of tags to content (e.g. suggestion-based)
User interface	Drag 'n Drop for placing content items on a page layout, Drag 'n Drop for uploading documents to the CMS, WYSIWYG-Editor for content authors, Undo, Redo
Content search	Facetted search (filtering of search results by categories), Search term suggestions when typing the query, Formal query language support (please provide details below)
Content modelling	Creation of a content type with a particular structure (e.g., for defining forms to be filled by end users, or defining presentation templates for specific kinds of information)
Performance features	Load Balancing, Page Caching, Static Content Export, Database Replication
Access restrictions	Document-level, Part-of-document-level, Group-level (role-level)

10.6 EPiServer AB, Sweden: EPiServer CMS

EPiSERVER

Management Summary

Web, e-Mail	www.episerver.com, info@episerver.com
Address	Regeringsgatan 67, 103 86 Stockholm, Sweden
CMS release	EPiServer CMS 6.0 (March 2010)
Number of employees	approx. 150
Branch offices	USA, UK, Sweden, Netherlands, Australia, South Africa, Denmark, Norway, Finland, Ukraine and Vietnam
Targeted customers	Medium and large enterprises
Reference customers	FIFA, Electrolux, Scandinavian Airlines
First version of CMS	1997
Short description of the CMS	EPiServer CMS is an all-encompassing site management platform where certain features and functionality will appeal more to specific roles; business owners, editors, marketers and developers focus on very different things. The guiding principle in developing EPiServer CMS is "Power through Simplicity". Powerful for the business owner and the editor with just a single sign-on to access the full range of EPiServer marketing tools or third party components, yet simple to ensure that organizations' digital initiatives can be brought to market rapidly.
	EPiServer CMS presents a modern user interface for today's business professionals. OnlineCenter's unified dashboard is a customizable workspace for day-to-day work. Business users can instantly access their work from anywhere via a browser, affording flexibility and control at all times.
	EPiServer CMS intuitive editing environment allows editors to maintain, change and update content, text, images, pages and workflows in an instant. They can localize content for different markets and set personalization features for different audiences. The many different functions and features include Dynamic content, Office integration, Page comparison, Image editing, Link checking, Globalization and Localization, all of which contribute to making it a very powerful authoring tool for editors who need to publish content online.
Licensing	Pricing for workstation license: Free to work with
	Pricing for server license: 9 000 EUR to 11 300 EUR 8 000 EUR is license and 1 000 EUR is subscription
	Trial: http://world.episerver.com (requires registration)

Overview of the CMS

Documentation of CMS	Web-based documentation and printed documentation for authors/editors, administrators and developers
Supported languages of the CMS	Chinese, English, French, German, Italian, Japanese, Portugese, Spanish, Dutch, Swedish, Norwegian, Finnish, Danish
Technical skills required for CMS use	Administrator: Basic understanding about web and how to set permissions Content author: Basic web knowledge
Time to learn to use the CMS	Administrator: 1 day training course Content author: 0.5 to 1 day training course
Service and support	E-Mail support, Phone support, On-site support, We only provide e-mail and phone support to our partners / developers. Pricing: email, phone and some on-site is free. Otherwise 150 EUR / hour

Supported Technologies

Operating systems	Microsoft Windows
Database management systems	Microsoft SQL Server, Oracle Database
Data formats	Database fields, XML, RDF, RDFa
Metadata models	Dublin Core (DC), Most of it can certainly be imple-mented fairly easy, but nothing out-of-the-box
Microformats	Microformats can be implemented, but nothing out-of-the-box
Database or knowledge representation languages	SQL
Query languages for content	SQL, XPath, XQuery
Indexing mechanisms	Apache Lucene
Rule / reasoning languages	n/a
Business process languages	n/a
Implementation languages	HTML, CSS, ASP, .NET, C, C#, C++
Presentation formats and mechanisms	HTML 4, HTML 5, XHTML, Flash, PDF, CSS, RSS, Text-to-audio, XSLT

CMS Features

Generic Interfaces	n/a
Interfaces to existing platforms	YouTube, Twitter and Facebook content, Notifica-tions to Twitter and Facebook
Support for content creation	n/a
Supported workflows	Supports a publication workflow with at least two CMS authors involved, Event-based triggering of emails, messages to Twitter and Facebook
Devices to access content	HTML client on desktop PC and mobile device, Native mobile application (Apple iPhone device in testing stage)
Devices to create content	HTML client on desktop PC, Native mobile application (Apple iPhone)
Personalization features	Personalized content author interface, Personalized end-user / consumer interface, Creation of personalized newsletters
Content enrichment	n/a
User interface	Drag 'n Drop for placing content items on a page layout, Drag 'n Drop for uploading documents to the CMS, WYSIWYG-Editor for content authors, Undo, Redo
Content search	Facetted search (filtering of search results by categories), Search term suggestions when typing the query
Content modelling	n/a
Performance features	Load Balancing, Page Caching, Static Content Export, Database Replication
Access restrictions	Document-level, Group-level (role-level)

10.7 Gentics Software GmbH, Austria: Gentics Content.Node

MANAGEMENT SUMMARY

Web, e-Mail	www.gentics.com, office@gentics.com
Address	Gonzagagasse 11/25, A-1010 Wien, Austria
CMS release	Gentics Content.Node 4.1 (July 2010)
Number of employees	approx. 23
Branch offices	Austria
Targeted customers	Large enterprises
Reference customers	D.Swarovski (all websites and portals, internal and external), Bundesrechenzentrum (operates many federal websites and portals), Erste Bank (E2.0 intranet for 55.000 employees)
First version of CMS	2000
Short description of the CMS	Gentics Content.Node is an easy to use Enterprise CMS system which is capable to manage a huge number of personalized content pages. It has staging and can publish static content, dynamic content and integrate into enterprise portal systems.
Licensing	Pricing for workstation license: only server-based Pricing for server license: on request, max. 30 000 EUR (unlimited); Pricing for ASP / Cloud license: same as server no special cloud version available Trial: http://demo-cms.gentics.com

OVERVIEW OF THE CMS

Documentation of CMS	Web-based documentation for authors/editors, administrators and developers
Supported languages of the CMS	English, German
Technical skills required for CMS use	Administrator: Linux, Mysql, tomcat, httpd Content author: Average PC knowledge
Time to learn to use the CMS	Administrator: 1.5 days Content author: 0.5 day
Service and support	E-Mail support, Phone support, Remote support, On-site support, Pricing: 3 different service levels. support price depends on license and level

SUPPORTED TECHNOLOGIES

Operating systems	Linux, Unix, Sun Solaris
Database management systems	Microsoft SQL Server, Oracle Database, Oracle MySQL
Data formats	Database fields
Metadata models	NewsML, Dublin Core (DC), Friend of a Friend (FOAF)
Microformats	hCard, hCalendar, hReview
Database or knowledge representation languages	SQL
Query languages for content	proprietary objects with an object based notation
Indexing mechanisms	Apache Lucene
Rule / reasoning languages	proprietary
Business process languages	n/a
Implementation languages	HTML, CSS, PHP, ASP, Java
Presentation formats and mechanisms	HTML 4, HTML 5, XHTML, Flash, PDF, CSS, RSS

CMS FEATURES

Generic Interfaces	n/a
Interfaces to existing platforms	YouTube, Twitter and Facebook content
Support for content creation	n/a
Supported workflows	Supports a publication workflow with at least two CMS authors involved, Event-based triggering of emails
Devices to access content	HTML client on desktop PC and mobile device
Devices to create content	HTML client on desktop PC
Personalization features	Personalized content author interface, Personalized end-user / consumer interface
Content enrichment	n/a
User interface	WYSIWYG-Editor for content authors, Undo, Redo
Content search	Facetted search (filtering of search results by categories)
Content modelling	Creation of a content type with a particular structure (e.g., for defining forms to be filled by end users, or defining presentation templates for specific kinds of information)
Performance features	Load Balancing, Page Caching, Static Content Export, Database Replication
Access restrictions	Part-of-document-level, Group-level (role-level), templates, files, objecttypes, attributes, language, administration, rights delegation, and more

10.8 GOSS Interactive Ltd, United Kingdom: GOSS iCM: intelligent Content Management

MANAGEMENT SUMMARY

Web, e-Mail	www.gossinteractive.com, enquiries@gossinteractive.com
Address	24 Darklake View, Plymouth, PL6 7TL, UK
CMS release	GOSS iCM 9.0.0.3 (December 2010)
Number of employees	approx. 50
Branch offices	UK
Targeted customers	Medium and large enterprises
Reference customers	Nottingham City Council, http://www.nottinghamcity.gov.uk Merseyside Police, http://www.merseyside.police.uk Brittany Ferries, http://www.brittanyferries.com/
First version of CMS	1998
Short description of the CMS	Our intelligent, next-generation technology allows the creation and management of Web 2.0 content rich websites. Publishing, workflows and concepts are supported by a comprehensive Content Management System that empowers multiple users, contributors and administrators. Key features: Accessibility validation, Bulk editing, Bulk uploading, Contributor assistance, Edit this page, Feature Groups, Forms, Friendly URLs, Group security layers, Image manipulation, Inlines, Mass email, Media usage tracking, Metadata, Scheduling, Search, Version history, Video support and training, Workflow, WYSIWYG. iSuggest selects topics from a given taxonomy of categories including IPSV (Integrated Public Sector Vocabulary) and other content such as documents. The iSuggest tool does this by automatically scanning digital content – and offering relevant metadata and other content for attachment.
Licensing	Pricing for workstation license: No client license; Pricing for server license: 12 000 EUR for single site license; Trial: Demo sites created when requested by potential customer.

10 CMS with No Particular Industry Focus 145

Overview of the CMS

Documentation of CMS	Web-based documentation for authors/editors, administrators and developers, printed handbook for authors/editors and administrators
Supported languages of the CMS	English
Technical skills required for CMS use	Administrator: Basic IT skills Content author: Basic keyboard skills
Time to learn to use the CMS	Administrator: 1 day training plus x days for certain areas Content author: 1 day training
Service and support	E-Mail support, Phone support, Remote support, On-site support and online forums, bi-annual user groups and regular webinars.

Supported Technologies

Operating systems	Microsoft Windows, Linux
Database management systems	Microsoft SQL Server, Oracle Database, PostgreSQL
Data formats	Database fields, XML, RDFa
Metadata models	Dublin Core (DC), Exchangeable Image File Format (EXIF), Integrated Public Sector Vocabulary (IPSV), Local Government Navigation List (LGNL).
Microformats	n/a
Database or knowledge representation languages	SQL
Query languages for content	SQL
Indexing mechanisms	Apache Solr
Rule / reasoning languages	n/a
Business process languages	n/a
Implementation languages	HTML, CSS, Java, .NET, C, C#, C++, Cold Fusion
Presentation formats and mechanisms	HTML 4, HTML 5, XHTML, Flash, PDF, CSS, RSS

CMS Features

Generic Interfaces	n/a
Interfaces to existing platforms	YouTube content, Twitter content, Facebook content, Notifications to Twitter, Notifications to Facebook
Support for content creation	Provides related links during content creation to the author, Provides related documents during content creation to the author, Provides related video clips during content creation to the author, iSuggest technology will auto-suggest related content and metadata
Supported workflows	Supports a publication workflow with at least two CMS authors involved, Event-based triggering of emails
Devices to access content	HTML client on desktop PC and mobile device
Devices to create content	HTML client on desktop PC and mobile device
Personalization features	Personalized content author interface, Personalized end-user / consumer interface, Creation of personalized newsletters
Content enrichment	iSuggest automatically suggests and relates content.
User interface	WYSIWYG-Editor for content authors, Undo, Redo, Version control, drag 'n drop interface for forms creation.
Content search	Facetted search (filtering of search results by categories), Search term suggestions when typing the query, Meta data driven searches
Content modelling	Creation of a content type with a particular structure (e.g., for defining forms to be filled by end users, or defining presentation templates for specific kinds of information)
Performance features	Load Balancing, Page Caching, Static Content Export, Granular caching of complex page elements
Access restrictions	Document-level, Group-level (role-level)

10.9 Homepage Toolbox, Austria: Homepage Toolbox

MANAGEMENT SUMMARY

Web, e-Mail	www.homepage-toolbox.com, mail@homepage-toolbox.com
Address	Doktor Leopold Groß Straße 5, 4840 Vöcklabruck, Austria
CMS release	Homepage Toolbox 3.0 (April 2010)
Number of employees	approx. 1
Branch offices	n/a
Targeted customers	Micro enterprises
Reference customers	Vita Med, Under Armour – Markus Möslinger, Pronto Pronto
First version of CMS	2005
Short description of the CMS	Homepage Toolbox is an easy-to-use server based CMS for rental. After ordering the customer gets a webserver with a ready installed Homepage Toolbox. The system contains a design editor, that writes valid CSS, so there is no need to create HTML templates. It uses AJAX Drag & Drop for sorting. A shop module is optional available.
Licensing	Pricing for server license: 49 EUR (Price per month for Standard Edition) Trial: demo.homepage-toolbox.com

OVERVIEW OF THE CMS

Documentation of CMS	n/a
Supported languages of the CMS	English, German
Technical skills required for CMS use	Administrator: None Content author: None
Time to learn to use the CMS	Administrator: Less than 1 day Content author: Less than 1 day
Service and support	E-Mail support

SUPPORTED TECHNOLOGIES

Operating systems	Linux
Database management systems	Oracle, MySQL
Data formats	Database fields
Metadata models	n/a
Microformats	n/a
Database or knowledge representation languages	SQL
Query languages for content	SQL
Indexing mechanisms	n/a
Rule / reasoning languages	n/a
Business process languages	n/a
Implementation languages	HTML, CSS, PHP
Presentation formats and mechanisms	XHTML, Flash, PDF, CSS, RSS

CMS FEATURES

Generic Interfaces	n/a
Interfaces to existing platforms	n/a
Support for content creation	n/a
Supported workflows	n/a
Devices to access content	n/a
Devices to create content	n/a
Personalization features	n/a
Content enrichment	n/a
User interface	Drag 'n Drop for placing content items on a page layout, WYSIWYG-Editor for content authors, Recycle Bin for deleted items
Content search	n/a
Content modelling	n/a
Performance features	n/a
Access restrictions	Group-level (role-level)

10.10 Jahia Solutions Group, Switzerland: Jahia

MANAGEMENT SUMMARY

Web, e-Mail	www.jahia.com, info@jahia.org
Address	Route des Jeunes, 9 1227 Geneve, Switzerland
CMS release	Jahia 6.4 (Quarter 4, 2010)
Number of employees	approx. 30
Branch offices	Switzerland, France, USA, Canada, Germany, Aus-tria
Targeted customers	Medium and large enterprises
Reference customers	United Nations, Auckland University (New Zealand), BUPA (United Kingdom)
First version of CMS	2002
Short description of the CMS	Jahia delivers the first Java, Open Source Web Content Integration Software by combining Enterprise Web Content Management with Document Management and Portal features. Jahia offers a complete solution for developing, integrating, delivering, and managing content across Intranets, Extranets, and the Internet.
Licensing	Pricing for server license and ASP / Cloud license: http://www.jahia.com/jahia/Jahia/Home/product/Pricing/euro No licence fee at all / open source model Trial: http: //www.jahia.com/jahia/Jahia/Home/product/download

Overview of the CMS

Documentation of CMS	Web-based documentation for authors/editors, administrators and developers
Supported languages of the CMS	English, French, German, Italian, Portugese, Spanish
Technical skills required for CMS use	Administrator: Java/app server knowledge. Networking protocols is a plus. Jahia training can help Content author: Jahia training, HTML and CSS is a plus but not mandatory
Time to learn to use the CMS	Administrator: 3 days Content author: 0.5 days
Service and support	E-Mail support, Phone support, Remote support, On-site support, Pricing: http://www.jahia.com/jahia/Jahia/Home/product/Pricing/euro

Supported Technologies

Operating systems	Microsoft Windows, Linux, Unix, Apple OS X, Amazon EC2
Database management systems	Microsoft SQL Server, Oracle Database, Oracle MySQL, PostgreSQL, Derby
Data formats	XML
Metadata models	NewsML, Dublin Core (DC)
Microformats	hCard, hCalendar
Database or knowledge representation languages	SQL, JCR Version 1 (JSR 170)
Query languages for content	SQL, XPath, XQuery
Indexing mechanisms	Apache Lucene, Apache SOLr, Nutch
Rule / reasoning languages	n/a
Business process languages	BPEL, jBPM, Drools
Implementation languages	HTML, CSS, Java, GWT, GXT
Presentation formats and mechanisms	HTML 4, XHTML, Flash, PDF, CSS, RSS, XSLT, 0.0

CMS Features

Generic Interfaces	JCR (JSR 170), JCR 2, Custom connectors and Content Hub to 30+ content repositories
Interfaces to existing platforms	YouTube and Twitter content, Notifications to Twitter and Facebook
Support for content creation	n/a
Supported workflows	Supports fundamental process primitives (e.g., forking, merging, choice points) for the specification of workflows by the CMS customer, Supports a publication workflow with at least two CMS authors involved, Event-based triggering of emails
Devices to access content	HTML client on desktop PC and mobile device
Devices to create content	HTML client on desktop PC
Personalization features	Personalized content author interface, Personalized end-user / consumer interface, Creation of personalized newsletters
Content enrichment	n/a
User interface	Drag 'n Drop for placing content items on a page layout, WYSIWYG-Editor for content authors, Change content object rendering in situation, display same content in several places with different renderings.
Content search	Facetted search (filtering of search results by categories), Search term suggestions when typing the query, Formal query language support
Content modelling	Creation of a content type with a particular structure (e.g., for defining forms to be filled by end users, or defining presentation templates for specific kinds of information)
Performance features	Load Balancing, Page Caching, Database Replication
Access restrictions	Document-level, Group-level (role-level)

10.11 Jarn AS, Norway: Plone

MANAGEMENT SUMMARY

Web, e-Mail	www.jarn.com, info@jarn.com
Address	Postboks 2236 NO-3103 Tønsberg, Norway
CMS release	Plone 4 (July, 2010)
Number of employees	approx. 12
Branch offices	Establishing in Germany fall 2010
Targeted customers	Medium enterprises
Reference customers	Beerenberg, Bergen public library, Elkjøp
First version of CMS	2003
Short description of the CMS	Plone is a powerful, flexible Content Management solution that is easy to install, use and extend Plone lets non-technical people create and maintain information using only a web browser. Perfect for web sites or intranets, Plone offers superior security without sacrificing extensibility or ease of use.
Licensing	No licence fee at all / open source model Trial: Full version is free and can be tested or used by anyone. http://plone.org/products/plone

Overview of the CMS

Documentation of CMS	Web-based documentation and printed handbooks for authors/editors, administrators and developers.
Supported languages of the CMS	Arabic, Chinese, English, French, German, Italian, Japanese, Portugese, Russian, Spanish, Turkish, Several others: see http://plone.org/documentation/faq/translations
Technical skills required for CMS use	Administrator: No technical skills needed for site administrators (as opposed to system administrators) Content author: No technical skills needed, infor-mation workers.
Time to learn to use the CMS	Administrator: 2 days Content author: 1 day training
Service and support	E-Mail support, Phone support, Remote support, On-site support, Consulting and maintenance services, Pricing for Support: 350 EUR / month

Supported Technologies

Operating systems	Microsoft Windows, Linux, Unix, Apple OS X, all major operating systems
Database management systems	Microsoft SQL Server, IBM DB2, Oracle Database, Oracle MySQL, PostgreSQL, Apache CouchDB, By default Plone uses an Object database (like the NoSQL hype), but supports all major RMDBSes for data storage when needed
Data formats	Database fields, XML
Metadata models	Dublin Core (DC)
Microformats	n/a
Database or knowledge representation languages	n/a
Query languages for content	ZCatalog Queries
Indexing mechanisms	Apache Lucene, Apache SOLr, Ships with ZCatalog. A lightweight alternative that works better for small sites. Large sites normally upgrade to SOLr.
Rule / reasoning languages	n/a
Business process languages	n/a
Implementation languages	HTML, CSS, Python
Presentation formats and mechanisms	HTML 4 and 5, XHTML, Flash, PDF, CSS, RSS, Text-to-audio, XSLT, 0.0

CMS Features

Generic Interfaces	Partial CMIS
Interfaces to existing platforms	YouTube, Twitter and Facebook content, No-tifications to Twitter and Facebook, Google docs, plenty other add-ons for integration
Support for content creation	n/a
Supported workflows	Supports a publication workflow with at least two CMS authors involved, Event-based triggering of emails and SMS messages
Devices to access content	HTML client on desktop PC and mobile device, Native desktop application (Integration with Windows Explorer/MS Office, Enfold desktop)
Devices to create content	HTML client on desktop PC and mobile device, Native desktop application (Integration with Windows Explorer/MS Office, Enfold desktop)
Personalization features	Personalized content author interface, Personalized end-user / consumer interface, Personal dashboards
Content enrichment	n/a
User interface	Drag 'n Drop for placing content items on a page layout, Drag 'n Drop for uploading documents to the CMS, WYSIWYG-Editor for content authors, Undo
Content search	Facetted search (filtering of search results by categories), Facetted search supported through add-ons with SOLR
Content modelling	Creation of a content type with a particular structure (e.g., for defining forms to be filled by end users, or defining presentation templates for specific kinds of information), Creation with UML and ArchGenXML code generator.
Performance features	Load Balancing, Page Caching, Static Content Export, Database Replication, static content export via add-on; database replication via ZRS (not open source) or DRBD / OpenAIS / Corosync (free)
Access restrictions	Document-level, Part-of-document-level, Group-level (role-level), Very fine grained security model: groups, roles, custom permissions, per-field (or method)-level permissions on content objects

10.12 Klein & Partner KG, BlueDynamics Alliance, Austria: Plone

MANAGEMENT SUMMARY

Web, e-Mail	www.kleinundpartner.at, office@kleinundpartner.at
Address	Grabenweg 68, 6020 Innsbruck, Austria
CMS release	Plone 4 (July 2010)
Number of employees	approx. 3
Branch offices	Austria, Germany, Switzerland
Targeted customers	Medium enterprises
Reference customers	http://www.beruf-und-familie.org (office Innsbruck), Zukunftszentrum Tirol http://www.bankenverband.de (office Cologne) http://faces.ch (office Zurich)
First version of CMS	2003
Short description of the CMS	A powerful, flexible Content Management Solution that is easy to install, use and extend. Plone lets non-technical people create and maintain information for a public website or an intranet using only a web browser. Plone is easy to understand and use – allowing users to be productive in just half an hour – yet offers a wealth of community-developed add-ons and extensibility to keep meeting your needs for years to come. Blending the creativity and speed of open source with a technologically advanced Python back-end, Plone offers superior security without sacrificing power or extensibility. Further Reading: http://plone.org/about
Licensing	No licence fee at all / open source model Trial: We provide a tailored dedicated test-install to customers.

Overview of the CMS

Documentation of CMS	Web-based documentation ad printed handbook for authors / editors, administrators and developers
Supported languages of the CMS	Arabic, Chinese, English, French, German, Italian, Japanese, Portugese, Russian, Spanish, Turkish, Plone is translated in over 40 languages, see `http://plone.org/documentation/faq/translations`
Technical skills required for CMS use	Administrator: basics in OS administration and webserver-management (for installation), good understanding of common possible CMS features helps (for configuration). Content author: computer basics, like ECDL, then Click and Create/Edit.
Time to learn to use the CMS	Administrator: 2 days Content author: 0.5 days
Service and support	E-Mail support, Phone support, Remote support, On-site support, pre-paid support possible, Pricing: depends on project

Supported Technologies

Operating systems	Microsoft Windows, Linux, Unix, Apple OS X, pre-ferred and most cost-efficient system is Debian GNU/Linux
Database management systems	ZODB (default database), all others can be integrated too, for most SQL-based databases add-ons are available.
Data formats	n/a
Metadata models	Dublin Core (DC), Exchangeable Image File Format (EXIF)
Microformats	n/a
Database or knowledge representation languages	n/a
Query languages for content	SQL, ZCatalog Queries
Indexing mechanisms	Apache Lucene, Apache SOLr, ZCatalog Indexes
Rule / reasoning languages	n/a
Business process languages	UML State Diagrams for Workflows as external add-on
Implementation languages	HTML, CSS, Python, C, C#, C++
Presentation formats and mechanisms	XHTML, PDF, CSS, RSS, XSLT

CMS Features

Generic Interfaces	Partial CMIS
Interfaces to existing platforms	YouTube, Twitter and Facebook content, Notifica-tions to Twitter and Facebook, all possible with add-ons
Support for content creation	n/a
Supported workflows	Supports a publication workflow with at least two CMS authors involved, Event-based triggering of emails, SMS messages, MMS messages, messages to Twitter and Facebook, Workflows for permission-management.
Devices to access content	HTML client on desktop PC and mobile device, Native desktop application, WebDAV, FTP
Devices to create content	HTML client on desktop PC and mobile device, WebDAV, FTP.
Personalization features	Personalized content author interface, Personalized end-user / consumer interface, Creation of personalized newsletters, dashboard
Content enrichment	n/a
User interface	Drag 'n Drop for placing content items on a page layout, Drag 'n Drop for uploading documents to the CMS, WYSIWYG-Editor for content authors, Undo, Redo
Content search	Facetted search (filtering of search results by categories), live-search, and different add-ons
Content modelling	Creation of a content type with a particular structure (e.g., for defining forms to be filled by end users, or defining presentation templates for specific kinds of information), Creation with UML and ArchGenXML code generator.
Performance features	Load Balancing, Page Caching, Static Content Export, Database Replication, static content export via add-on; database replication via ZRS (not open source) or DRBD / OpenAIS / Corosync (free)
Access restrictions	Document-level, Part-of-document-level, Group-level (role-level), Very fine grained security model: groups, roles, custom permissions, per-field (or method)-level permissions on content objects

10.13 Magnolia International Ltd., Switzerland: Magnolia CMS

MANAGEMENT SUMMARY

Web, e-Mail	www.magnolia-cms.com, info-us@magnolia-cms.com
Address	St.Johanns-Vorstadt 38, 4056 Basel, Switzerland
CMS release	Magnolia CMS 4.3 (March 2010)
Number of employees	approx. 25
Branch offices	Switzerland, USA, Czech Republic, Spain
Targeted customers	Large enterprises
Reference customers	LoveFilm U.K., Texas State University, Sony Computer Entertainment Europe
First version of CMS	Open source version: 2003, commercial version: 2006
Short description of the CMS	Magnolia is easy-to-use yet enterprise-grade software that is highly scalable, follows industry standards, runs on Java, and is available both as a free Open-Source Community Edition and a supported commercial Enterprise Edition. Magnolia provides a very rich out-of-the-box publishing environment yet is extremely open and flexible to be used in myriad different use cases. It has a distributed architecture, is built on JSR-170, the Java Content Repository API, has a built-in module mechanism, a highly customizable and powerful workflow engine, can manage unstructured, semi-structured and structured data, includes security and caching mechanisms and can manage multi-site, multi-language and multi-domain environments.
Licensing	Pricing for server license: 8 500 EUR (subscription per year). No licence fee at all / open source model Trial: http://www.magnolia-cms.com/home/top-level/download.html

Overview of the CMS

Documentation of CMS	Web-based documentation for authors / editors, ad-ministrators and developers
Supported languages of the CMS	Arabic, Chinese, English, French, German, Italian, Japanese, Portugese, Russian, Spanish, others
Technical skills required for CMS use	Administrator: standard Java deployment skills Content author: Understand how to use a keyboard and a web browser
Time to learn to use the CMS	Administrator: 1 to 5 days Content author: 1 to 2 days
Service and support	E-Mail support, Remote support, On-site support, Pricing: included in subscription

Supported Technologies

Operating systems	Microsoft Windows, Linux, Unix, Apple OS X
Database management systems	Microsoft SQL Server, IBM DB2, Oracle Database, Oracle MySQL, PostgreSQL, Apache CouchDB, Ingres etc.
Data formats	Database fields, XML, hierarchical data structures
Metadata models	Dublin Core (DC), any custom meta data structures can easily be declared at runtime
Microformats	hCard, hCalendar
Database or knowledge representation languages	SQL, JCR Version 1 (JSR 170)
Query languages for content	SQL, XPath
Indexing mechanisms	Apache Lucene
Rule / reasoning languages	n/a
Business process languages	OpenWFE
Implementation languages	HTML, CSS, Java, JavaScript, Freemarker, JSP
Presentation formats and mechanisms	HTML 4 and 5, XHTML, CSS, RSS, any output can be generated by using custom templates

CMS Features

Generic Interfaces	JCR (JSR 170)
Interfaces to existing platforms	YouTube and Twitter content, custom templates make such integrations possible
Support for content creation	n/a
Supported workflows	Supports fundamental process primitives (e.g., forking, merging, choice points) for the specification of workflows by the CMS customer, Supports a publication workflow with at least two CMS authors involved, Event-based triggering of emails, messages to Twitter and Facebook (Twitter / Facebook messaging custom, examples exist)
Devices to access content	HTML client on desktop PC and mobile device
Devices to create content	HTML client on desktop PC and mobile device, Mobile support is restricted but will fully work with next major release
Personalization features	Personalized content author interface, Personalized end-user / consumer interface, Creation of personalized newsletters, personalization on delivery is custom but easily possible depending on needs
Content enrichment	n/a
User interface	Drag 'n Drop for placing content items on a page layout, WYSIWYG-Editor for content authors, Undo, Redo
Content search	n/a
Content modelling	Creation of a content type with a particular structure (e.g., for defining forms to be filled by end users, or defining presentation templates for specific kinds of information)
Performance features	Load Balancing, Page Caching, Database Replication
Access restrictions	Document-level, Part-of-document-level, Group-level (role-level), up to node data level if needed

10.14 MASSIVE ART WebServices GmbH, Austria: ZOOLU

MA**SSIVE**ART

MANAGEMENT SUMMARY

Web, e-Mail	www.massiveart.com, www.getzoolu.org, webservices@massiveart.com
Address	Arlbergstrasse 115, 6900 Bregenz, Austria
CMS release	ZOOLU 1.0 (July 2010)
Number of employees	approx. 12
Branch offices	Austria
Targeted customers	Micro, small and medium enterprises
Reference customers	Ivoclar Vivadent, Neutrik AG, Collini
First version of CMS	2009
Short description of the CMS	ZOOLU is an open source content management system (CMS) for creating, editing and publishing content in a website. The software is built upon technologies such as PHP5, mySQL and Zend Framework. The development is strictly object oriented and uses a generic database model.
	The main focus of ZOOLU is the development of large scale and multi-portal websites. Administrators can create the navigation and content of a website or portal completely generic. The design of a site can be controlled via templates. ZOOLU also provides multi language support for the CMS and the published content.
	By using the built-in SEO functionalities such as the flexible and user-controlled URL-rewriting, websites can be easily optimized for search engines. The modular user interface of the CMS is fully web based and has been developed to provide the highest level of usability as possible. In particular the multi-column navigation tree allows a very easy administration of web pages.
Licensing	No licence fee at all / open source model Trial: playground.getzoolu.org, playground.getzoolu.org/zoolu

Overview of the CMS

Documentation of CMS	Web-based documentation for authors / editors and administrators
Supported languages of the CMS	English, German
Technical skills required for CMS use	Administrator: basic PHP knowledge for site admin, advanced for customization through content admins Content author: no specific skills needed
Time to learn to use the CMS	Administrator: 1 to 2 days Content author: 1 day
Service and support	E-Mail support

Supported Technologies

Operating systems	Linux
Database management systems	Oracle MySQL
Data formats	Database fields
Metadata models	n/a
Microformats	n/a
Database or knowledge representation languages	SQL
Query languages for content	SQL
Indexing mechanisms	Apache Lucene
Rule / reasoning languages	n/a
Business process languages	n/a
Implementation languages	HTML, CSS, PHP
Presentation formats and mechanisms	HTML 4, HTML 5, XHTML, PDF, CSS, RSS

CMS Features

Generic Interfaces	n/a
Interfaces to existing platforms	YouTube content, Twitter content, Vimeo
Support for content creation	n/a
Supported workflows	n/a
Devices to access content	HTML client on desktop PC
Devices to create content	HTML client on desktop PC
Personalization features	Personalized content author interface, Personalized end-user / consumer interface
Content enrichment	n/a
User interface	WYSIWYG-Editor for content authors
Content search	n/a
Content modelling	n/a
Performance features	Page Caching
Access restrictions	Document-level, Group-level (role-level)

10.15 Modera, Estonia: Modera Webmaster

MANAGEMENT SUMMARY

Web, e-Mail	www.modera.com, info@modera.net
Address	Laki 25, 12915 Tallinn, Estonia
CMS release	Modera Webmaster / Pro., / Ent. 5.04.0 (August 2010)
Number of employees	approx. 70
Branch offices	26 countries, including USA, UK and Hong Kong
Targeted customers	Micro, small, medium and large enterprises
Reference customers	Nissan Europe, HMV / Mama Group PLC, Citizen Watches Co
First version of CMS	2001
Short description of the CMS	Visioning, universal work-flow, module development standard (MMDK) tagging, ajax driven user friendly interface, modular build, application exchange, SEO tools, keyword generator, change management.
Licensing	Pricing for workstation license depends on the model (user-based and URL-based licences); Pricing for server license depends on the product), Pricing for ASP/ Cloud license: approx. 50 EUR Trial: www.modera.com/modera-webmaster/cms/demo

OVERVIEW OF THE CMS

Documentation of CMS	Web-based documentation and printed handbooks for authors / editors, administrators and developers
Supported languages of the CMS	Arabic, Chinese, English, French, German, Italian, Japanese, Portugese, Russian, Spanish, Turkish, 32 world languages
Technical skills required for CMS use	Administrator: None Content author: None
Time to learn to use the CMS	Administrator: 1 to 2 days Content author: 1 day
Service and support	E-Mail support, Phone support, Remote support, On-site support, Local partners and resellers support their customers

SUPPORTED TECHNOLOGIES

Operating systems	Microsoft Windows, Linux, Unix, Apple OS X
Database management systems	Microsoft SQL Server, IBM DB2, Oracle Database, Oracle MySQL, PostgreSQL, Apache CouchDB, MySQL
Data formats	Database fields, XML, RDF, RDFa, New platform supports all + CMIS
Metadata models	n/a
Microformats	n/a
Database or knowledge representation languages	SQL
Query languages for content	SQL
Indexing mechanisms	Apache Lucene
Rule / reasoning languages	n/a
Business process languages	n/a
Implementation languages	HTML, CSS, PHP
Presentation formats and mechanisms	HTML 4, HTML 5, XHTML, Flash, PDF, CSS, RSS, XSLT

CMS Features

Generic Interfaces	CMIS 1.0
Interfaces to existing platforms	YouTube, Twitter and Facebook content, Notifica-tions to Twitter and Facebook
Support for content creation	n/a
Supported workflows	Supports fundamental process primitives (e.g., forking, merging, choice points) for the specification of workflows by the CMS customer, Supports a publication workflow with at least two CMS authors involved, Event-based triggering of emails, SMS messages, MMS messages, FAX messages, messages to Twitter and Facebook
Devices to access content	HTML client on desktop PC and mobile device
Devices to create content	HTML client on desktop PC and mobile device
Personalization features	Personalized content author interface, Personalized end-user / consumer interface, Creation of personalized newsletters
Content enrichment	Semi-automated creation of links for named entities (e.g., recognition of a city and creation of a Link to Wikipedia), Automated creation of links for named entities, Semi-automated creation of tags to content (e.g. suggestion-based), Automated creation of tags to content
User interface	Drag 'n Drop for placing content items on a page layout, Drag 'n Drop for uploading documents to the CMS, WYSIWYG-Editor for content authors, Undo, Redo
Content search	Facetted search (filtering of search results by categories), Search term suggestions when typing the query
Content modelling	Creation of a content type with a particular structure (e.g., for defining forms to be filled by end users, or defining presentation templates for specific kinds of information)
Performance features	Load Balancing, Page Caching, Static Content Export, Database Replication
Access restrictions	Document-level, Part-of-document-level, Group-level (role-level)

10.16 Nemein Oy, Finland: Midgard CMS

MANAGEMENT SUMMARY

Web, e-Mail	`http://nemein.com`, `sales@nemein.com`
Address	Hietalahdenkatu 8 A 22, 00180 Helsinki, Finland
CMS release	Midgard2 10.05.3 (February 2011)
Number of employees	approx. 10
Branch offices	Finland
Targeted customers	Small to large enterprises
Reference customers	Amer Sports Corporation VTI Technologies HL Group
First version of CMS	2001
Short description of the CMS	Midgard2 is a content repository. It provides an object-oriented and replicated environment for building data-intensive applications. This provides several advantages: • Common rules for data access mean that multiple applications can work with same content without breaking consistency of the data • Signals about changes let applications know when another application using the repository modifies something, enabling collaborative data management between apps • Objects instead of SQL mean that developers can deal with data using APIs more compatible with the rest of their desktop programming environment, and without having to fear issues like SQL injection, etc. Midgard's philosophy includes building on top of a well-known and supported GNOME libraries like glib and libgda on the system end, and connecting with popular programming languages like PHP and Python. Data storage can utilize SQLite with desktop and mobile applications, or a database server like MySQL or Postgres for web application storage.
Licensing	No licence fee at all / open source model: GNU Lesser General Public License (LGPL) Trial: `http://www.midgard-project.org/download/`

Overview of the CMS

Documentation of CMS	Web-based documentation for authors/editors, administrators and developers
Supported languages of the CMS	Database with existing i18n exists, but not accessible
Technical skills required for CMS use	Administrator: PHP
Time to learn to use the CMS	Administrator: 2 to 3 days Content author: 1 to 2 days
Service and support	E-Mail support, phone, remote and on-site support

Supported Technologies

Operating systems	Linux, Apple OS X
Database management systems	Oracle MySQL
Data formats	Database fields
Metadata models	n/a
Microformats	n/a
Database or knowledge representation languages	SQL
Query languages for content	SQL
Indexing mechanisms	n/a
Rule / reasoning languages	n/a
Business process languages	n/a
Implementation languages	HTML, PHP, Python, C, C#, C++
Presentation formats and mechanisms	HTML 4

CMS Features

Generic Interfaces	n/a
Interfaces to existing platforms	Drupal, LDAP, Active Directory for authentication
Support for content creation	n/a
Supported workflows	n/a
Devices to access content	HTML client on desktop PC and mobile device
Devices to create content	Native desktop application
Personalization features	n/a
Content enrichment	n/a
User interface	WYSIWYG-Editor for content authors, Undo, Redo
Content search	n/a
Content modelling	n/a
Performance features	Database Replication
Access restrictions	Document-level, Part-of-document-level, Group-level (role-level)

10.17 NexxaCon IT-Consulting GmbH, Austria: join2learn

NexxaCon

Management Summary

Web, e-Mail	www.nexxacon.com, info@nexxacon.com
Address	Robert-Fuchs-Strasse 44, 8053 Graz, Austria
CMS release	join2learn 2.3 (September 2010)
Number of employees	approx. 2
Branch offices	Austria
Targeted customers	Medium and large enterprises
Reference customers	n/a
First version of CMS	n/a
Short description of the CMS	Join2learn is one platform for knowledge management and e-Learning. It is an Asset-based Content Management System with e-Learning functionalities. Each content can be stored in any language. The copyrights of the authors are considered and each content could have its own access rights.
Licensing	Pricing for workstation license: on request; Pricing for server license: 400 EUR per month (incl. 50 users / small to medium companies); Pricing for ASP / Cloud license: on request

Overview of the CMS

Documentation of CMS	Web-based documentation and printed handbook for authors / editors and administrators, web-based documentation for developers
Supported languages of the CMS	English, German, Thai
Technical skills required for CMS use	Administrator: none Content author: none
Time to learn to use the CMS	Administrator: 1 day Content author: 1 day
Service and support	E-Mail support, Phone support

SUPPORTED TECHNOLOGIES

Operating systems	Microsoft Windows, Linux
Database management systems	Microsoft SQL Server, Oracle Database, Oracle MySQL
Data formats	Database fields, XML
Metadata models	n/a
Microformats	n/a
Database or knowledge representation languages	JCR Version 1 (JSR 170)
Query languages for content	XPath, XQuery
Indexing mechanisms	Apache Lucene
Rule / reasoning languages	n/a
Business process languages	n/a
Implementation languages	HTML, CSS, Java
Presentation formats and mechanisms	HTML 4, XHTML, Flash, PDF, CSS

CMS FEATURES

Generic Interfaces	JCR (JSR 170)
Interfaces to existing platforms	n/a
Support for content creation	n/a
Supported workflows	Supports a publication workflow with at least two CMS authors involved, Event-based triggering of emails
Devices to access content	HTML client on desktop PC
Devices to create content	HTML client on desktop PC
Personalization features	Personalized content author interface, Personalized end-user / consumer interface
Content enrichment	Automated creation of tags to content
User interface	Drag 'n Drop for placing content items on a page layout, WYSIWYG-Editor for content authorsn
Content search	n/a
Content modelling	n/a
Performance features	Load Balancing, Page Caching
Access restrictions	Document-level, Part-of-document-level, Group-level (role-level)

10.18 Nuxeo, France: NUXEO

nuxeo

MANAGEMENT SUMMARY

Web, e-Mail	www.nuxeo.com, contact@nuxeo.com
Address	18 rue Soleillet, Paris, France
CMS release	NUXEO 5.4.0 (November 2010)
Number of employees	approx. 50
Branch offices	France, USA
Targeted customers	Small enterprises
Reference customers	Agence France Presse, Leroy Merlin, Serrimax
First version of CMS	2003
Short description of the CMS	Nuxeo is a comprehensive free software / open source Enterprise Content Management (ECM) platform. It has been designed to be robust, scalable and highly extensible, by using modern open source Java EE technologies, such as: the JCR, JSF, EJB3, JBoss Seam, OSGi, and a Service Oriented Approach. It can be used to develop both web-based server applications and Rich Client applications. It currently covers the following functions of the ECM spectrum: • Document management (DM) • Collaborative Work • Business process management (workflow) • Compliance • Records management • Digital asset management (DAM) • Case management
Licensing	Pricing for workstation and server license: Open source; Pricing for ASP / Cloud license: 5 000 EUR (see http://www.nuxeo.com/en/subscription/ecm-cloud/pricing); No licence fee at all / open source model Trial: http://www.nuxeo.com/en/downloads

Overview of the CMS

Documentation of CMS	Web-based documentation for authors / editors, ad-ministrators and developers
Supported languages of the CMS	Arabic, Chinese, English, French, German, Italian, Japanese, Portugese, Russian, Vietnamese, Catalan, Basque
Technical skills required for CMS use	Administrator: Know-how to install server software Content author: Knows how to use a word-processor
Time to learn to use the CMS	Administrator: 2 days Content author: 1 day
Service and support	E-Mail support, Phone support, Remote support, `http://www.nuxeo.com/en/subscription/connect/pricing`

Supported Technologies

Operating systems	Microsoft Windows, Linux, Unix, Apple OS X
Database management systems	Microsoft SQL Server, Oracle Database, Oracle MySQL, PostgreSQL
Data formats	XML
Metadata models	NewsML, Dublin Core (DC)
Microformats	n/a
Database or knowledge representation languages	SQL
Query languages for content	SQL, CMISQL
Indexing mechanisms	SOLr support coming up in next release
Rule / reasoning languages	n/a
Business process languages	jBPM
Implementation languages	HTML, CSS, Java
Presentation formats and mechanisms	HTML 4, HTML 5, XHTML, CSS, RSS

CMS Features

Generic Interfaces	CMIS 1.0
Interfaces to existing platforms	n/a
Support for content creation	n/a
Supported workflows	Supports fundamental process primitives (e.g., forking, merging, choice points) for the specification of workflows by the CMS customer, Supports a publication workflow with at least two CMS authors involved, Event-based triggering of emails
Devices to access content	HTML client on desktop PC and mobile device, Native mobile application (iOS, Windows Mobile and Android)
Devices to create content	HTML client on desktop PC
Personalization features	Personalized dashboard
Content enrichment	n/a
User interface	Drag 'n Drop for uploading documents to the CMS
Content search	Search term suggestions when typing the query
Content modelling	Creation of a content type with a particular structure (e.g., for defining forms to be filled by end users, or defining presentation templates for specific kinds of information)
Performance features	Load Balancing, Static Content Export, Database Replication
Access restrictions	Group-level (role-level)

10.19 Ooffee, France: Apache Lenya

MANAGEMENT SUMMARY

Web, e-Mail	`www.ooffee.eu, florent.andre@ooffee.eu`
Address	54 rue de Conflans, 94220 Charenton le pont, France
CMS release	Apache Lenya 2.0.3 (January 2010)
Number of employees	approx. 1
Branch offices	France
Targeted customers	Small, medium and large enterprises
Reference customers	`http://lenya.apache.org/community/live-sites.html` EDF R&D, France
First version of CMS	2000
Short description of the CMS	Apache Lenya is an Open Source Java/XML Content Management System and comes with revision control, multi-site management, scheduling, search, WYSIWYG editors, and workflow. Key features: • Standard compliance by default (XHTML 1.0) • Ability to use any (even yours) xml format and process it • Authoring • Workflow • Internationalization • Layout • Site Management • Security Details for each item: `http://lenya.apache.org`
Licensing	No licence fee at all / open source model Trial: `http://lenya.zones.apache.org:9999/`

Overview of the CMS

Documentation of CMS	Web-based documentation for authors / editors, ad-ministrators and developers
Supported languages of the CMS	Arabic, Chinese, English, French, German, Italian, Japanese, Portuguese, Russian, Spanish, Turkish, Not all languages are fully supported, but Lenya is easy to translate in any language
Technical skills required for CMS use	Administrator: Most is done by GUI, just a little bit of XML for advanced configuration Content author: Not any, just know how to use an editor like word
Time to learn to use the CMS	Administrator: 5 days Content author: 1 to 2 days
Service and support	E-Mail support, Phone support, Remote support

Supported Technologies

Operating systems	Microsoft Windows, Linux, Unix, Apple OS X
Database management systems	Microsoft SQL Server, Oracle MySQL, PostgreSQL, Apache CouchDB, any database supported by JDBC
Data formats	Database fields, XML, RDF
Metadata models	Dublin Core (DC), Friend of a Friend (FOAF), Simple Knowledge Organisation System (SKOS), As Lenya can deal with any XML format, just a module and some configuration have to be done for support on format.
Microformats	n/a
Database or knowledge representation languages	SQL, JCR, OWL and RDF are in the pipe for the next version
Query languages for content	SQL, XPath, XQuery
Indexing mechanisms	Apache Lucene, SOLr is in the pipe for the next version
Rule / reasoning languages	n/a
Business process languages	n/a
Implementation languages	HTML, CSS, Java, XML
Presentation formats and mechanisms	XHTML, Flash, PDF, CSS, RSS, XSLT, XML

CMS Features

Generic Interfaces	CMIS 1.0
Interfaces to existing platforms	n/a
Support for content creation	Planned integration of IKS FISE
Supported workflows	Supports fundamental process primitives (e.g., forking, merging, choice points) for the specification of workflows by the CMS customer, Supports a publication workflow with at least two CMS authors involved, Event-based triggering of emails
Devices to access content	HTML client on desktop PC and mobile device
Devices to create content	HTML client on desktop PC and mobile device
Personalization features	Personalized content author interface, Personalized end-user / consumer interface, Creation of personalized newsletters, Document rendering: Lenya use and XLST pipe processing concept allows to personalize each content rendering
Content enrichment	In the pipe for new version with IKS FISE integration
User interface	Drag 'n Drop for uploading documents to the CMS, WYSIWYG-Editor for content authors, Undo, Redo
Content search	Search term suggestions when typing the query
Content modelling	Creation of a content type with a particular structure (e.g., for defining forms to be filled by end users, or defining presentation templates for specific kinds of information), For each XML format we can define a particular way to fill
Performance features	Load Balancing, Page Caching, Static Content Export
Access restrictions	Document-level, Group-level (role-level), user level and function level

10.20 punkt. netServices GmbH, Austria: conX

MANAGEMENT SUMMARY

Web, e-Mail	www.punkt.at, office@punkt.at
Address	Lerchenfelder Gürtel 43, A-1160 Wien, Austria
CMS release	conX 2.5 (2010)
Number of employees	approx. 10
Branch offices	n/a
Targeted customers	Small and medium enterprises
Reference customers	REEEP, Know Center Graz, Red Cross Austria / ACCORD
First version of CMS	2000
Short description of the CMS	conX 2.5 is an XML based technology framework for the professional and efficient development of web-based IT solutions as knowledge portals, community environments, project-management tools or company websites.
Licensing	Pricing: TCO – model, only customisation needs to be paid Trial: http://www.conx.biz/index.php?id=1&content=demo

OVERVIEW OF THE CMS

Documentation of CMS	Web-based documentation for authors / editors and administrators
Supported languages of the CMS	English, French, German
Technical skills required for CMS use	Administrator: Internet skills as usual Content author: Internet skills as usual
Time to learn to use the CMS	Administrator: 0.5 to 1 days Content author: 3 to 5 hours
Service and support	E-Mail support, Phone support, Remote support, On-site support, Pricing: depends on the respective contract

Supported Technologies

Operating systems	Linux
Database management systems	Oracle MySQL, PostgreSQL
Data formats	Database fields, XML, RDF
Metadata models	n/a
Microformats	n/a
Database or knowledge representation languages	SQL, RDF Schema
Query languages for content	SQL, SPARQL
Indexing mechanisms	Lucene
Rule / reasoning languages	n/a
Business process languages	n/a
Implementation languages	HTML, CSS, PHP
Presentation formats and mechanisms	HTML 4, XHTML, PDF, CSS, XSLT

CMS Features

Generic Interfaces	n/a
Interfaces to existing platforms	n/a
Support for content creation	n/a
Supported workflows	Supports fundamental process primitives (e.g., forking, merging, choice points) for the specification of workflows by the CMS customer, Supports a publication workflow with at least two CMS authors involved
Devices to access content	HTML client on desktop PC and mobile device
Devices to create content	HTML client on desktop PC
Personalization features	Personalized end-user / consumer interface, Creation of personalized newsletters, personalisation in community environments depending on project requirements
Content enrichment	n/a
User interface	WYSIWYG-Editor for content authors, Undo, Redo
Content search	Facetted search (filtering of search results by categories), moderated search on basis of thesaurus (suggestions for query expansions)
Content modelling	Creation of a content type with a particular structure (e.g., for defining forms to be filled by end users, or defining presentation templates for specific kinds of information)
Performance features	Page Caching, Database Replication
Access restrictions	Document-level

10.21 semsol, Germany: Paggr CMS

MANAGEMENT SUMMARY

Web, e-Mail	www.semsol.com, bnowack@semsol.com
Address	Bielefelder Str. 5, 40468 Düsseldorf, Germany
CMS release	Paggr CMS (May 2010)
Number of employees	approx. n/a
Branch offices	Germany
Targeted customers	n/a
Reference customers	n/a
First version of CMS	2010
Short description of the CMS	Paggr CMS is a widget-based system where each widget is generated from local or remote RDF data repositories and sources.
Licensing	Pricing for server license: approx. 490 EUR Trial: on request

OVERVIEW OF THE CMS

Documentation of CMS	n/a
Supported languages of the CMS	English, German, the UI can be localized
Technical skills required for CMS use	Administrator: LAMP setup, PHP-based configurations, FTP Content author: basic IT skills
Time to learn to use the CMS	n/a
Service and support	E-Mail support, Phone support, Remote support, custom theme and module development, installation and setup, Pricing: 90 EUR per hour

SUPPORTED TECHNOLOGIES

Operating systems	Microsoft Windows, Linux, Unix, Apple OS X
Database management systems	Oracle MySQL
Data formats	RDF, RDFa
Metadata models	Dublin Core (DC), Friend of a Friend (FOAF), Semantically-Interlinked Online Communities (SIOC), Simple Knowledge Organisation System (SKOS), any RDF-based model
Microformats	hCard, hCalendar, hReview, xfolk, hResume, hAtom, XFN
Database or knowledge representation languages	OWL, RDF Schema
Query languages for content	SPARQL
Indexing mechanisms	MySQL fulltext indexes
Rule / reasoning languages	SPARQL script, SPARQL update
Business process languages	n/a
Implementation languages	HTML, CSS, PHP, JavaScript
Presentation formats and mechanisms	HTML 5, XHTML, CSS, RSS, RDF formats (Microdata, Turtle, RDF / XML, etc.)

CMS FEATURES

Generic Interfaces	SPARQL protocol
Interfaces to existing platforms	via modules
Support for content creation	Related links and related documents during content creation (planned)
Supported workflows	n/a
Devices to access content	HTML client on desktop PC and mobile device
Devices to create content	HTML client on desktop PC
Personalization features	n/a
Content enrichment	Semi-automated creation of links for named entities (e.g., recognition of a city and creation of a Link to Wikipedia), Semi-automated creation of tags to content (e.g., suggestion-based) (planned)
User interface	Drag 'n Drop for placing content items on a page layout, WYSIWYG-Editor for content authors, Undo, Redo
Content search	Facetted search (filtering of search results by categories), Formal query language support (please provide details below), via modules, SPARQL
Content modelling	Creation of a content type with a particular structure (e.g., for defining forms to be filled by end users, or defining presentation templates for specific kinds of information)
Performance features	Load Balancing, Page Caching, Database Replication, DB replication needs custom code
Access restrictions	module-level

Chapter 11
CMS with a Particular Industry Focus

11.1 CIC Creative Internet Consulting GmbH, Germany: packagemaster®

Touristik.Internet.Erfolg.

MANAGEMENT SUMMARY

Web, e-Mail	www.packagemaster.de, info@cic.de
Address	Europa-Allee 5, 64625 Bensheim, Germany
CMS release	packagemaster 2.1 (September 2010)
Number of employees	approx. 23
Branch offices	Germany
Targeted customers	Small enterprises
Industry focus	Tourism
Reference customers	IKARUS TOURS GmbH, www.ikarus.com Phoenix Reisen GmbH, www.phoenixreisen.com Mediplus REISEN, www.mediplusreisen.de
First version of CMS	2003
Short description of the CMS	Today, packagemaster® is used by 68 companies in the tourist branch. They use packagemaster® for the publication of their product data in PRINT & WEB. packagemaster® is used for the media-neutral management of product information (texts, tables, selectable features, photos, graphs, documents). All media channels can be outputted specifically according to market and affiliation from a single system. With packagemaster® you can produce Catalogue pages, Websites, Print advertising of all kinds, Mail-ings and Newsletters. Data export to external sys-tems. With one and the same system, you can control your websites and sales campaigns including newsletter centrally. Using the page planner in the print module, you can build up complete catalogue sections and output these in high layout quality using the robot function.
Licensing	Pricing for workstation license: n/a Pricing for server license (approx.): 30 000 EUR Pricing for ASP/ Cloud license (approx.): 300 EUR

Overview of the CMS

Documentation of CMS	Printed handbook for authors/editors and administrators
Supported languages of the CMS	English, German
Technical skills required for CMS use	Administrator: n/a Content author: n/a
Time to learn to use the CMS	Administrator: 1 day Content author: 1 day
Service and support	E-Mail support, Phone support, Only on request

Supported Technologies

Operating systems	Microsoft Windows
Database management systems	Microsoft SQL Server
Data formats	Database fields, XML
Metadata models	n/a
Microformats	n/a
Database or knowledge representation languages	SQL
Query languages for content	SQL
Indexing mechanisms	n/a
Rule / reasoning languages	n/a
Business process languages	n/a
Implementation languages	HTML, CSS
Presentation formats and mechanisms	HTML 4, PDF

CMS Features

Generic Interfaces	n/a
Interfaces to existing platforms	n/a
Support for content creation	n/a
Supported workflows	Event-based triggering of emails
Devices to access content	HTML client on Desktop PC
Devices to create content	HTML client on Desktop PC
Personalization features	Creation of personalized newsletters
Content enrichment	n/a
User interface	n/a
Content search	Facetted search (filtering of search results by categories)
Content modelling	n/a
Performance features	Database Replication
Access restrictions	Group-level (role-level)

11.2 Hippo B.V., The Netherlands: Hippo CMS

MANAGEMENT SUMMARY

Web, e-Mail	www.onehippo.com, sales@onehippo.com
Address	Oosteinde 11, 1017 WT Amsterdam, The Netherlands
CMS release	Hippo CMS 7.4 (July 2010)
Number of employees	approx. 55
Branch offices	The Netherlands, United States of America
Targeted customers	Medium and large enterprises
Industry focus	Government, publishing, medical, knowledge-intensive organizations
Reference customers	Dutch government (www.rijksoverheid.nl), University of Southern California, Dolce&Gabbana
First version of CMS	Pricing for workstation license: n/a; Pricing for server license: 12 500 EUR (Support subscription per year); Pricing for ASP / Cloud license: 4 000 EUR (per month); No licence fee at all / open source model; Trial: http://www.onehippo.org/cms7/documentation/quickstart.html installer version available from August 1st 2010 at www.onehippo.com
Short description of the CMS	Hippo CMS 7 is a user-friendly open source content management system designed to deliver enterprise level performance and reliability. Hippo CMS focuses on content reuse and multi-channel publishing. It features a user-friendly interface including a modern AJAX GUI with tabbed editing and auto-save functionality. Hippo CMS 7 is highly standardized and extensible and includes a wide variety of plug-ins enabling an organization to satisfy their particular requirements for managing and utilizing their enterprise content. This flexible architecture allows developers to easily add custom functionality.
Licensing	Pricing for workstation license: n/a Pricing for server license (approx.): 30 000 EUR Pricing for ASP/ Cloud license (approx.): 300 EUR

Overview of the CMS

Documentation of CMS	Web-based documentation and printed handbook for Authors/Editors, web-based documentation for administrators and developers
Supported languages of the CMS	English, Italian, Dutch
Technical skills required for CMS use	Administrator: n/a Content author: n/a
Time to learn to use the CMS	Administrator: 2 days Content author: 0.5 days (through train-the-trainer)
Service and support	E-Mail support, Phone support, Remote support, On-site support, Pricing: Starts at 12.500 EUR

Supported Technologies

Operating systems	Microsoft Windows, Linux, Unix, Apple OS X, Server is Java-based, platform independent. Client is browser based, all major browsers supported.
Database management systems	Microsoft SQL Server, Oracle Database, Oracle, MySQL
Data formats	XML, RDFa
Metadata models	Dublin Core (DC), Exchangeable Image File Format (EXIF)
Microformats	n/a
Database or knowledge representation languages	JCR Version 1 (JSR 170)
Query languages for content	SQL, XPath
Indexing mechanisms	Apache Lucene
Rule / reasoning languages	n/a
Business process languages	jBPM
Implementation languages	HTML, CSS, Java
Presentation formats and mechanisms	HTML 4, HTML 5, XHTML, Flash, PDF, CSS, RSS, XSLT

CMS Features

Generic Interfaces	JCR (JSR 170), WebDAV, REST
Interfaces to existing platforms	YouTube content, Twitter content
Support for content creation	Provides related links and documents during content creation to the author
Supported workflows	Supports a publication workflow with at least two CMS authors involved, Event-based triggering of emails
Devices to access content	HTML client on Desktop PC
Devices to create content	HTML client on Desktop PC
Personalization features	Personalized content author interface, Personalized end-user / consumer interface, Creation of personalized newsletters
Content enrichment	Semi-automated creation of links for named entities (e.g., recognition of a city and creation of a Link to Wikipedia), Semi-automated creation of tags to content (e.g. suggestion-based), Automated creation of tags to content
User interface	WYSIWYG-Editor for content authors, Undo, Working on first 3 points
Content search	Facetted search (filtering of search results by categories), Search term suggestions when typing the query
Content modelling	Creation of a content type with a particular structure (e.g., for defining forms to be filled by end users, or defining presentation templates for specific kinds of information)
Performance features	Load Balancing, Page Caching, Database Replication
Access restrictions	Document-level, Group-level (role-level)

11.3 PAUX Technologies GmbH, Germany: PAUX

MANAGEMENT SUMMARY

Web, e-Mail	www.paux.de, info@paux.de
Address	Schönhauser Allee 42, 10435 Berlin, Germany
CMS release	PAUX (2010)
Number of employees	approx. 2
Branch offices	Germany
Targeted customers	Large enterprises
Industry focus	Publishing houses and content providers
Reference customers	Springer Science+Business Media, Deutsches Zentrum für Luft- und Raumfahrt (DLR, German Aerospace), Juristisches Repetitorium Hemmer
First version of CMS	2006
Short description of the CMS	PAUX is a Microcontent Management System. It stores single words in a database, links them to sen-tences, sentences to paragraphs etc. Objects and relationships in PAUX can be valuated: for a certain target group with a certain previous knowledge the object or relationship has a certain relevancy, difficulty and quality.
Licensing	Pricing for workstation license: 3 000 EUR Pricing for server license: 15 000 EUR Pricing for ASP / Cloud license: 3 000 EUR In general: costs depend on project Trial: https://paux.com:8443/deploy/paux.jnlp

Overview of the CMS

Documentation of CMS	Web-based documentation for Authors/Editors, Web-based documentation for Administrators, Web-based documentation for Developers
Supported languages of the CMS	English, German, other languages if requested
Technical skills required for CMS use	Administrator: n/a Content author: n/a
Time to learn to use the CMS	Administrator: 1-2 Content author: 0.5
Service and support	E-Mail support, Phone support, Remote support

Supported Technologies

Operating systems	Microsoft Windows, Linux, Unix, Apple OS X, Solaris
Database management systems	PostgreSQL, adaption if required
Data formats	Database fields, XML, RDF
Metadata models	NewsML, Dublin Core (DC), Friend of a Friend (FOAF), Simple Knowledge Organisation System (SKOS), adaption if required
Microformats	n/a
Database or knowledge representation languages	SQL, JCR Version 1 (JSR 170), OWL, RDF Schema
Query languages for content	SPARQL, OQL (Object Query Language)
Indexing mechanisms	Apache Lucene, Apache SOLr
Rule / reasoning languages	n/a
Business process languages	BPML, BPEL, jBPM, Drools
Implementation languages	HTML, CSS, Java, NetReXX
Presentation formats and mechanisms	HTML 4 and 5, XHTML, PDF, CSS, RSS, XSLT, XSL-FO

CMS Features

Generic Interfaces	n/a
Interfaces to existing platforms	YouTube, Twitter and Facebook content, notifications to Twitter and Facebook under development
Support for content creation	n/a
Supported workflows	Supports fundamental process primitives (e.g., forking, merging, choice points) for the specification of workflows by the CMS customer, Supports a publication workflow with at least two CMS authors involved, Event-based triggering of emails, Event-based triggering of SMS, MMS and fax messages, Event-based triggering of messages to Twitter and Facebook
Devices to access content	HTML client on Desktop PC, Native desktop application (Java Swing)
Devices to create content	HTML client on Desktop PC, Native desktop application (Java Swing)
Personalization features	Personalized content author interface, Personalized end-user / consumer interface, Creation of personalized newsletters
Content enrichment	Automated creation of links for named entities
User interface	WYSIWYG-Editor for content authors, Undo, Redo
Content search	Facetted search (filtering of search results by categories), Formal query language support (OQL)
Content modelling	Creation of a content type with a particular structure (e.g., for defining forms to be filled by end users, or defining presentation templates for specific kinds of information)
Performance features	Load Balancing, Page Caching, Database Replication, Syncing Offline-Servers
Access restrictions	Document-level, Part-of-document-level, Group-level (role-level), any entity possible

11.4 QuinScape GmbH, Germany: OpenSAGA

MANAGEMENT SUMMARY

Web, e-Mail	www.quinscape.de, info@quinscape.de
Address	Wittekindstr. 30, 44139 Dortmund, Germany
CMS release	OpenSAGA 1.5.1 (December 2010)
Number of employees	approx. 48
Branch offices	Germany
Targeted customers	Large enterprises
Industry focus	Government
Reference customers	On request
First version of CMS	2008
Short description of the CMS	OpenSAGA is an open-source software platform that supports the efficient development of modern web applications. The OpenSAGA platform has been optimized to considerably simplify the design of SAGA-compliant and Java-based web applications and provides unique features which support the generation and development of government and local authority IT systems, specifically in the e-government sector.
Licensing	No licence fee at all; Trial: provided on request; Commercial add-on application modules available

OVERVIEW OF THE CMS

Documentation of CMS	Web-based documentation for Authors/Editors, Printed Handbook for Authors/Editors, Web-based documentation and printed handbook for administrators and developers
Supported languages of the CMS	English, German, Completely adaptable to other languages
Technical skills required for CMS use	Administrator: XML, Java App Server administration (Tomcat as the baseline)
Time to learn to use the CMS	Administrator: 0.5 to 2 days Content author: 0.5 to 5 days
Service and support	E-Mail support, Phone support, Remote support, On-site support, forums, Pricing: Depends on the particular SLA

Supported Technologies

Operating systems	Microsoft Windows, Linux, Unix, Apple OS X
Database management systems	Ingres, Microsoft SQL Server, Oracle Database, PostgreSQL, MySQL, HSQLDB
Data formats	Database fields, XML, Excel
Metadata models	n/a
Microformats	n/a
Database or knowledge representation languages	SQL, Custom integration interfaces available for arbitrary persistence layers
Query languages for content	SQL, XPath, XQuery, Custom integration interfaces available for arbitrary query languages
Indexing mechanisms	n/a
Rule / reasoning languages	n/a
Business process languages	n/a
Implementation languages	Java, Ruby, Python, Groovy, BeanShell
Presentation formats and mechanisms	HTML 4, HTML 5, XHTML, PDF, CSS, RSS, XSLT, 1.0

CMS Features

Generic Interfaces	n/a
Interfaces to existing platforms	Notifications to Twitter
Support for content creation	n/a
Supported workflows	Completely customizable, so basically all of the above, but requiring some customization
Devices to access content	HTML client on desktop PC and mobile device
Devices to create content	HTML client on desktop PC and mobile device
Personalization features	Personalized content author interface, Personalized end-user / consumer interface, Portlets
Content enrichment	Programmatic Apache Stanbol integration available
User interface	WYSIWYG-Editor for content authors
Content search	Based on database queries, complex data filters
Content modelling	Creation of a content type with a particular structure (e.g., for defining forms to be filled by end users, or defining presentation templates for specific kinds of information)
Performance features	Load Balancing
Access restrictions	Document-level, Part-of-document-level, Group-level (role-level), Object-level, Field-level

11.5 TERMINALFOUR, Ireland: TERMINALFOUR: Site Manager

MANAGEMENT SUMMARY

Web, e-Mail	www.terminalfour.com, info@terminalfour.com
Address	110 Amiens Street, Dublin 1, Ireland
CMS release	TERMINALFOUR Site Manager 7.0.6 (August 2010)
Number of employees	approx. 50
Branch offices	Ireland, UK, North America
Targeted customers	Medium and large enterprises
Industry focus	Higher Education, Government, Retail & Finance
Reference customers	UNAIDS, Aviva Insurance, University of Manchester
First version of CMS	1999
Short description of the CMS	TERMINALFOUR is a leading provider of highly functional Enterprise Web Content Management Systems, eForms and Self Service software and associated professional services. Our open platform software enables organisations to improve the creation, flow and delivery of information through various channels including Web sites, personalised portals, intranets, extranets and utilising emerging technologies. The company has a strong presence within the Higher Education, Government, Retail and Finance sectors.
Licensing	Pricing for workstation license: n/a Pricing for server license: We do not license based on servers but on volume of content. Pricing for ASP / Cloud license: Available on request Trial: A demo environment can be setup according to the potential client's needs.

Overview of the CMS

Documentation of CMS	Web-based documentation for Authors/Editors, Web-based documentation for Administrators, Web-based documentation for Developers
Supported languages of the CMS	Arabic, Chinese, English, French, German, Italian, Japanese, Portugese, Russian, Spanish, Irish, Welsh
Technical skills required for CMS use	Administrator: HTML-Scripting languages to take advantage of more advanced features (minimum) Content author: Basic keyboard skills
Time to learn to use the CMS	Administrator: 2 days for a Web Master, 5 days for a Software Developer. Content author: 0.5 days is recommended
Service and support	E-Mail support, Phone support, Remote support, On-site support, Pricing: Based on a percentage of license fee.

Supported Technologies

Operating systems	Microsoft Windows, Linux, Unix, Apple OS X
Database management systems	Microsoft SQL Server, Oracle Database, Oracle MySQL, PostgreSQL
Data formats	Database fields, XML, RDF, RDFa
Metadata models	NewsML, Dublin Core (DC), Friend of a Friend (FOAF), Semantically-Interlinked Online Communities (SIOC), Exchangeable Image File Format (EXIF), Simple Knowledge Organisation System (SKOS), GoodRelations Product Ontology, Smart Product Description Object (SPDO), eGSM, ESD & IPSMS
Microformats	hCard, hCalendar, hReview, VoteLinks
Database or knowledge representation languages	SQL
Query languages for content	SQL, XPath, XQuery
Indexing mechanisms	Apache Lucene
Rule / reasoning languages	n/a
Business process languages	n/a
Implementation languages	HTML, CSS, PHP, ASP, Java, .NET, C, C#, C++
Presentation formats and mechanisms	HTML 4, HTML 5, XHTML, Flash, PDF, CSS, RSS, Text-to-audio, XSLT, no restriction on output format

11 CMS with a Particular Industry Focus

CMS Features

Generic Interfaces	CMIS 1.0, Partial support for JSR 170
Interfaces to existing platforms	YouTube, Twitter and Facebook content, Notifications to Twitter and Facebook
Support for content creation	Provides related links, documents and video clips during content creation to the author
Supported workflows	Supports fundamental process primitives (e.g., forking, merging, choice points) for the specification of workflows by the CMS customer, Supports a publication workflow with at least two CMS authors involved, Event-based triggering of emails, SMS messages and messages to Twitter and Facebook
Devices to access content	HTML client on desktop PC and mobile device
Devices to create content	HTML client on desktop PC and mobile device
Personalization features	Personalized content author interface, Personalized end-user / consumer interface
Content enrichment	Semi-automated creation of links for named entities (e.g., recognition of a city and creation of a Link to Wikipedia), Automated creation of links for named entities, Semi-automated creation of tags to content (e.g. suggestion-based), Automated creation of tags to content
User interface	Drag 'n Drop for placing content items on a page layout, Drag 'n Drop for uploading documents to the CMS, WYSIWYG-Editor for content authors, Undo, Redo
Content search	Facetted search (filtering of search results by categories), Search term suggestions when typing the query
Content modelling	Creation of a content type with a particular structure (e.g., for defining forms to be filled by end users, or defining presentation templates for specific kinds of information)
Performance features	Load Balancing, Page Caching, Static Content Export
Access restrictions	Document-level, Part-of-document-level, Group-level (role-level)

11.6 TXT Polymedia, Italy: TXT Polymedia

MANAGEMENT SUMMARY

Web, e-Mail	www.txtgroup.com, info@txtgroup.com
Address	via Frigia 27, 20126 Milano, Italy
CMS release	TXT Polymedia 6 (2010)
Number of employees	approx. 500
Branch offices	n/a
Targeted customers	Medium and large enterprises
Industry focus	Newspapers, TV Broadcasters, Telcos
Reference customers	Mediaset, Telecom Italia, RCS MediaGroup
First version of CMS	n/a
Short description of the CMS	TXT Polymedia is a software product featuring in one unique integrated system, advanced functions for Web Content Management, Multichannel Content Delivery and Media Asset Management. It is a complete software suite allowing to manage the whole life-cycle of rich contents and video: acquisition from heterogeneous sources, multilayer archiving and searching, multimedia editing, video transcoding and DRM protection, publishing on a variety of channels and devices (Web, WebTV, IPTV, Mobile VAS, Mobile TV, DTT and Teletext).
Licensing	On request

OVERVIEW OF THE CMS

Documentation of CMS	Web-based documentation and printed handbook for authors/editors, administrators and developers
Supported languages of the CMS	English, Italian
Technical skills required for CMS use	Administrator: Advanced computer literacy and media knowledge Content author: Standard computer literacy
Time to learn to use the CMS	Administrator: 3 days Content author: 2 days
Service and support	E-Mail support, Phone support, Remote support, On-site support

11 CMS with a Particular Industry Focus

SUPPORTED TECHNOLOGIES

Operating systems	Microsoft Windows, Linux, Unix
Database management systems	Microsoft SQL Server, IBM DB2, Oracle Database
Data formats	Database fields, XML, RDF
Metadata models	NewsML, Dublin Core (DC), Exchangeable Image File Format (EXIF)
Microformats	n/a
Database or knowledge representation languages	SQL
Query languages for content	SQL, XPath, XQuery
Indexing mechanisms	Apache Lucene
Rule / reasoning languages	n/a
Business process languages	Proprietary workflow engine
Implementation languages	HTML, CSS, ASP, Java, C, C#, C++
Presentation formats and mechanisms	HTML 4, HTML 5, XHTML, Flash, PDF, CSS, RSS, Text-to-audio, XSLT, Teletext, SMS, MMS

CMS FEATURES

Generic Interfaces	n/a
Interfaces to existing platforms	YouTube and Facebook content, Notifications to Facebook
Support for content creation	n/a
Supported workflows	Supports fundamental process primitives (e.g., forking, merging, choice points) for the specification of workflows by the CMS customer, Supports a publication workflow with at least two CMS authors involved, Event-based triggering of emails, SMS and MMS messages, and messages to Twitter and Facebook
Devices to access content	HTML client on desktop PC and mobile device, Native desktop and mobile applications
Devices to create content	n/a
Personalization features	n/a
Content enrichment	n/a
User interface	Undo, Redo
Content search	n/a
Content modelling	Creation of a content type with a particular structure (e.g., for defining forms to be filled by end users, or defining presentation templates for specific kinds of information)
Performance features	Database Replication
Access restrictions	Document-level, Part-of-document-level, Group-level (role-level)

Index

Accessibility, 65, 66, 70, 71
AI, 78
Algorithm, 14, 39, 77, 83
    machine-learning, 28
    mapping, 46
    matching, 38
    search, 38, 78
    semantic, 29
    semantic annotation, 39
Analysis
    concept, 55
    sentiment, 27
Annotation, 40, 43–46, 54, 56, 61, 64, 70, 71
    automatic, 93
    content, 55
    semantic, 4, 35, 39, 40, 44, 45, 51, 54, 65, 66
    text, 25
Application
    contextual, 24, 31
    crossover, 25
    enterprise, 25
    knowledge-based, 75
    semantic, 23–25, 27, 29–33, 92, 104
    web-based, 76
Artificial Intelligence (AI), 4, 76, 77
Association, 73
    semantic, 55
Authorization, 13, 18

BI, 26
BPEL, 114
BPML, 114
Business Intelligence (BI), 6
Business Process Management, 6

Categorization, 16

Classification, 27, 69
    dynamic, 29
Classification schema, 26
CMIS, 115
CMS
    commercial, 5
    corporate, 3
    cross media, 4
    eLearning, 4
    Enterprise, 4, 6
    JCR-based, 38
    modern, 12
    non-commercial, 5
    online, 4
    semantic, 24, 36, 37, 91, 93–95, 97, 99, 101, 103, 105, 107
    traditional, 35, 50, 92
    web, 4
Collaborative tagging, 71
Commerce
    real-time, 5
Communication
    corporate, 3, 22
    online, 3
Communication Management, 3
Content
    3D, 6
    archival, 16
    contextually relevant, 12
    digital, 3, 4, 6, 76
    meaningful, 6
    mobile, 6
    relational, 49
    relevant, 18
    semantic, 93
    semi-structured, 30, 40
    similar, 18, 37

smart, 23, 27
structured, 30
unstructured, 4, 30, 31, 40, 41
user-adaptive, 6
user-generated, 37, 47
Content mining, 47
Content syndication, 25
Context-awareness, 28
Curation, 16
  explicit, 16
  implicit, 16

Data
  big, 5, 6
  personal, 6
  semantic, 99, 100
  semi-structured, 47
  sensor, 6
  structured, 23, 98, 100
  unstructured, 4, 23
Data federation, 25
Database
  relational, 4, 47, 53–56, 76, 83, 99, 103
DBPedia, 56, 96–99, 103, 112
Deep Web, 4, 23–25
Description
  semantic, 4, 69, 71, 92, 96, 98
  structured, 4
Description logic, 82
Drools, 114
DSP, 49–51, 55, 60–62
Dublin Core (DC), 4, 69, 114
Dynamic Semantic Publishing (DSP), 49–51, 53, 55, 57, 59, 61, 63

eBusiness, 83
eCommerce, 29, 111
Editorial team, 13
Editorial workforce, 11–13, 15, 17, 19, 21
  decentralized, 12
eGovernment, 6, 65–73
Entity
  LOD, 94–98
  named, 116
  semantic, 15, 39, 98, 100
Entity extraction, 15, 27
Evaluation, 111, 113, 115, 117, 119, 121, 123
Exchangeable Image File Format (EXIF), 114
Expert System, 76

Faceted navigation, 29
Faceted search, 116
FISE, 38–40, 43–47, 89, 95, 97
Folksonomy, 66

Freebase, 24
Friend of a Friend (FOAF), 114
Furtwangen IKS Semantic Engine (FISE), 38

GeoNames, 56
GoodRelations Product Ontology, 114
Graph theory, 54

IKS, 33, 42, 46, 47, 75–77, 79–81, 83–90, 92, 94, 97, 99, 101, 102, 105, 107
In-line editing, 13
  role-based, 13
Inference, 49, 59, 61, 65, 100, 101, 104
Information
  categorial, 14
  contextual, 18
  related, 18
  semantic, 40, 94, 97
  structured, 79
  taxonomic, 14, 15
  unstructured, 24–26
Information hub, 24
Information retrieval, 66, 80
Information Warehouse
  smart, 24
  trusted, 24
Information warehouse, 25, 30
Infrastructure
  cloud, 6
  mobile, 6
  stationary, 6
Intelligence
  collective, 25
  content, 28
  data, 28
Interaction, 12
  3D, 6
  knowledge-based, 84, 85
Interactive Knowledge Stack, 75, 77, 79, 81, 83, 85, 87, 89, 93
Interactive Knowledge Stack (IKS), 84, 89, 92, 105, 111, 112
Internet Movie Database, 15, 24
Interoperability, 65–71, 93, 97, 101

Java Content Repository API (JCR), 35
jBPM, 114
JCR, 35–45, 47, 48, 86

Keyword, 14, 16, 24, 27
Knowledge discovery, 66
Knowledge management, 107
Knowledge Representation and Reasoning Support (KReS), 93, 101

Knowledge Representation Language (KRL), 81
KReS, 93, 97–99, 101–104
KRL, 81, 82

Language detection, 36
Lingua franca, 21
Linked Data, 27, 49, 69, 76, 89, 93, 100, 105
Linked Open Data (LOD), 56, 64, 76, 82, 93
LOD, 56, 59, 64, 91, 94–98, 100
LOD cloud, 98, 100
Long tail, 3

Market
  advertising, 5
  big data, 5, 6
  business, 5
  CMS, 4
  long-tail, 5
  private, 5
Metadata, 12, 25, 26, 29, 40, 50, 51, 54–58, 60–62, 64, 67, 69–71, 79
  semantic, 35, 36, 38, 40, 43, 47, 54
  taxonomic, 14
Microformat, 4, 100, 112
Micropayment, 16
Model Driven Architecture, 68
Model View Controller (MVC), 53

Natural Language Processing (NLP), 97, 105
Natural Language Technology, 30
Network effect, 11
NLP, 105

Object Request Broker (ORB), 77
Ontology, 6, 49, 55–58, 60, 61, 66, 69, 81, 83, 86, 87, 91, 93, 98–103, 105, 107
  domain, 55–57, 59
  heavy-weight, 68, 70
Ontology network, 101–103
Ontology pattern, 91, 97, 99, 100, 105
Open Directory Project, 15
Open Innovation, 5
Open Source, 5, 51, 84, 87, 113
ORB, 77
OSGi, 46, 75, 85, 89, 97
OWL, 26, 56, 60, 82, 83, 93, 98–100, 103, 104, 112, 114

Peer-to-Peer (P2P), 69
Permission, 12, 18
Presentation
  contextual, 14, 18
Privacy, 71, 81, 82

Protocol, 21
Public Relations, 22
Publishing
  dynamic, 61
  semantic, 25

Qwiki, 26

RDBMS, 64, 103
RDF, 4, 26, 39, 40, 43, 45, 46, 49, 56, 59–61, 64, 67, 75, 82, 83, 86, 89, 91, 93, 96–105, 112, 114
RDF Schema, 64, 114
RDFa, 4, 93, 114
Reasoning, 54, 56–58, 64, 82, 83, 85, 86, 91–93, 99–102, 104, 105
Reasoning language, 114
Relational Database Management System (RDBMS), 53
Remote Procedure Call (RPC), 77
Repository, 46, 97
  content, 37, 41, 44, 46, 47
  data, 6
Reputation, 14, 18–21
Reputation quotient, 19, 20
Reputation score, 19, 20
Reputation system, 20
Resource Description Framework (RDF), 4, 49
RIF, 104, 114
Right, 14, 18, 19, 21
Role, 13, 14, 16, 18–21
RPC, 77
RSS, 53, 100, 103, 114
Rule, 11, 15, 37, 50, 82, 91, 94, 96–101, 103, 104
  entity extraction, 15
  execute, 99
  integrity, 96
  logic, 93, 99, 100
  mapping, 99
  syntactic, 82
  transformation, 99
  validity, 96–99
Rule Interchange Format (RIF), 97
Rule language, 114

SA-WSDL, 71
SAN, 53
SBA, 29, 30
Search, 3, 4, 36, 37, 51, 77–80
  semantic, 70, 75
Search Based Application (SBA), 29
Search engine, 4, 24, 49, 76, 78, 79
Search Engine Optimization (SEO), 15, 79

Search index
  distributed, 4
  federated, 4
Security, 4, 6
Semantic industry, 29
Semantic navigation, 50, 55
Semantic query, 40, 44, 45
Semantic similarity, 38
Semantic Web, 24, 25, 30, 32, 76, 81–83, 86, 93, 94, 97, 104, 105, 107
Semantic web service, 82
Semantically-Interlinked Online Communities (SIOC), 114
Semantics
  compositional, 82
  computational, 6
  lexical, 82, 83
SEO, 15, 79
Service-oriented Architecture (SOA), 69, 77
Silo
  content, 6, 7, 26
  information, 24
Simple Knowledge Organisation System (SKOS), 99, 114
Smart Product Description Object (SPDO), 114
SOA, 69, 77
Social bookmarking, 72
Social media, 3, 5, 75, 79, 80
Social network, 23, 71, 81
Spam, 37
SPARQL, 26, 40, 45, 56, 59–62, 64, 104, 112, 114
Spell checker, 36
SQL, 54, 59, 64, 114
Storage Area Network (SAN), 53
Surf-and-edit, 13
SWRL, 93, 104, 112, 114

Tag, 6, 37, 70, 116
Tag cloud, 72
Taxonomy, 6, 15, 66, 69, 98, 99
Tool
  annotation, 61
  content analysis, 26
  curation, 16
  editing, 17
  query, 35
  semantic, 11, 14, 21, 29, 35, 47, 65
  semantic image analysis, 38
  text analysis, 26
Triple store, 40, 56, 59–62, 83, 86, 89, 91, 100, 101

UI, 51, 53, 55, 61
UML Use Case diagram, 94, 95
Usability, 76
User experience, 25, 26, 29, 32, 49
User interface (UI), 36, 40, 51, 116
User-generated content, 37

Vocabulary, 54, 93, 98–100, 103
  controlled, 54

Web 2.0, 37, 47, 71
Web 3.0, 24
Web Service Modeling Ontology, 69
WebGL, 6
Wikipedia, 3, 4, 24, 25, 37, 39, 116
Wordnet, 4
Workflow, 11, 18, 20, 51, 55
  editorial, 22
  organic, 12

XPath, 114
XQuery, 61, 62, 114

Printed by Publishers' Graphics LLC